THE ATLANTIC CRITICAL STUDIES

Salman Rushdie's

Midnight's Children

THE ATLANTIC CRITICAL STUDIES

Salman Rushdie's *Midnight's Children*

Pradip Kumar Dey

ATLANTIC
PUBLISHERS & DISTRIBUTORS (P) LTD

Published by
ATLANTIC
PUBLISHERS & DISTRIBUTORS (P) LTD
7/22, Ansari Road, Darya Ganj, New Delhi-110002
Phones : +91-11-40775252, 23273880, 23275880, 23280451
Fax : +91-11-23285873
Web : www.atlanticbooks.com
E-mail : orders@atlanticbooks.com

Branch Office
5, Nallathambi Street, Wallajah Road, Chennai-600002
Phones : +91-44-64611085, 32413319
E-mail : chennai@atlanticbooks.com

Printed in India at Nice Printing Press, A-33/3A, Site-IV, Industrial Area, Sahibabad, Ghaziabad, U.P.

General Preface

The Atlantic Critical Studies are study-aids modelled on the study-aids available in England and America, among other places, and are primarily meant for the students of English Literature of Indian universities.

However, in consideration of the local conditions and the various constraints under which our students have to study—non-availability of relevant critical books, dearth of foreign and Indian journals, inaccessibility to good, well-equipped libraries, just to mention a few of them—the models have been considerably improved upon, both qualitatively and quantitatively.

Thus, while these studies are meant to be comprehensive and self-sufficient, the distinguished scholars who have prepared these study materials, have taken special care to combine lucidity and profundity in their treatment of the texts.

The Select Bibliography at the end is meant not only to acknowledge the sources used but also to help a student in the pursuit of further studies if s/he wants to.

Atlantic Publishers & Distributors (P) Ltd., believe in quality and excellence. These studies will only reconfirm it.

MOHIT K. RAY
Chief Editor [English Literature]
Atlantic Publishers & Distributors (P) Ltd.,
New Delhi

General Preface

Preface

Salman Rushdie remains a major Indian writer in English. His birth coincides with the birth of a new modern nation on August 15, 1947. He has been justly labeled by the critics as a post-colonial writer who knows his trade well. His second novel *Midnight's Children* was published in 1981 and it raised a storm in the hitherto middle class world of fiction writing both in English and in vernaculars. While the great masters of Indian English writing, Raja Rao and R.K. Narayan tried to uphold in their fiction the mainstream politics and purity of Brahmanical order, Rushdie for the first time burst into the world of fiction with subversive themes like impurity, illegitimacy, plurality and hybridity. He understands that a civilization called India exists at many levels and that the vast landscape called India may be profitably understood as a dream, a collage of many colours, a blending of cultures and nationalities, a pluralistic society and in no way unitary.

In his epical novel *Midnight's Children*, he speaks of many Indians and many versions of reality. High seriousness of the elderly writers, in his fiction, is replaced by playfulness, comicality and trivialization. *Midnight's Children* remains an Indian novel in the sense that the author delves deep into Indian psyche and unearths rich reservoir of ancient indigenous resources like epic, folklore, myths and rituals which till the day, inform the mind and belief system of the millions in a substantial way. To know the mind of the sub-continent one should know the archetypal mythical figure of Ganesh and his large elephantine nose and ears. The urge for largeness, bigness exemplifies one typical Indian mindset, a desire for the whole. The narrator hero of the novel *Midnight's Children*, Saleem

Sinai is the proponent of this Indian mindset, and proclaims, "To understand just one life, you have to swallow the world."

Midnight's Children remains an impure text because the protagonists are of illegitimate birth and Saleem has four fathers and three mothers in a fairy-tale fashion. Though a post-modern text, the hero Saleem does not suffer from alienation, nor does he feel an exile in a society of teeming millions who jostle in and around him. Alienated self is an absurdity in an Indian context where a sensitive soul cannot afford exilic status *vis-à-vis* abundance, multiplicity, plurality, diverse customs and mores which exercise a magnetic spell on his mind. After Rushdie, Indian fiction is not what it was. The succeeding generation of Indian writers of fiction finds in Rushdie a guru of the post-colonial times and more and more Indian writers of English show their concern for community, nation, society and so on. It may be said, and said rightly, that with Rushdie, Indian English fiction comes of age. *Midnight's Children* remains a classic of post-colonial Indian writing, a novel of novels.

The present book constitutes a modest attempt at understanding the mind and art of a genius, as I understand, of our time. Any error in judgment or treatment of issues is absolutely mine.

Pradip Kumar Dey

Contents

1

Salman Rushdie—Life, Works and Achievements

Salman Rushdie was born in Bombay (now Mumbai) on 19 June 1947. He went to school in Bombay and at Rugby in England, and read History at King's College, Cambridge, where he joined the Cambridge Footlights Theatre Company. After graduating, he lived with his family who had moved to Pakistan in 1964, and worked briefly in television before returning to England, beginning work as a copywriter for an advertising agency. His first novel *Grimus* was published in 1975.

His second novel, the acclaimed *Midnight's Children*, was published in 1981. It won the Booker Prize for Fiction, the James Tait Black Memorial Prize (for fiction), an Arts Council Writers' Award and the English-Speaking Union Award, and in 1993 was judged to have been the 'Booker of Bookers,' the best novel to have won the Booker Prize for Fiction in the award's 25-year history. The novel narrates key events in the history of India through the story of a pickle-factory worker Saleem Sinai, one of 1001 children born as India won independence from Britain in 1947. The critic Malcolm Bradbury acclaimed the novel's achievement in *The Modern British Novel* (Penguin, 1994): 'a new start for the late-twentieth-century novel.'

Rushdie's third novel, *Shame* (1983), which many critics saw as an allegory of the political situation in Pakistan, won the Prix du Meilleur Livre Étranger and was shortlisted for the Booker Prize for Fiction. The publication in 1988 of his fourth novel, *The Satanic Verses*, led to accusations of blasphemy against Islam by the Islamist groups in India and Pakistan. The orthodox Iranian leadership issued a *fatwa* against Rushdie on 14 February 1989, effectively a sentence of death—and he was forced into hiding under the protection of the British government and police. The book itself centres on the adventures of two Indian actors, Gibreel and Saladin, who fall to earth in Britain when their Air India jet explodes. It won the Whitbread Novel Award in 1988.

Salman Rushdie continued to write and publish books, including a children's book, *Haroun and the Sea of Stories* (1990), a warning about the dangers of storytelling and won the Writers' Guild Award (Best Children's Book), and which he adapted for the stage (with Tim Supple and David Tushingham. It was first staged at the Royal National Theatre, London.). Then followed a book of essays entitled *Imaginary Homelands: Essays and Criticism 1981-1991* (1991); *East West* (1994), a book of short stories; and a novel, *The Moor's Last Sigh* (1995), the history of the wealthy Zogoiby family told through the story of Moraes Zogoiby, a young man from Bombay descended from Sultan Muhammad XI, the last Muslim ruler of Andalucia.

The Ground Beneath Her Feet, published in 1999, re-works the myth of Orpheus and Eurydice in the context of modern popular music. His most recent novel, *Fury*, set in New York at the beginning of the third millennium, was published in 2001. He is also the author of a travel narrative, *The Jaguar Smile* (1987), an account of a visit to Nicaragua in 1986.

Salman Ruishdie is Honorary Professor in the Humanities at the Massachusetts Institute of Technology (MIT), and Fellow of the Royal Society of Literature. He was made Distinguished Fellow in Literature at the University of East Anglia in 1995. He was awarded the Austrian State Prize for European Literature in 1993 and the European Union Aristeion Prize in 1996, and has received eight honorary doctorates. He was elected to the Board of American PEN in 2002. The subjects in his new book, *Step Across This Line: Collected Non-fiction 1992-2002* (2002), range from popular culture and football to twentieth-century literature and politics. Salman Rushdie is also co-author (with Tim Supple and Simon Reade) of the stage adaptation of

Midnight's Children, premiered by the Royal Shakespeare Company in 2002.

Selected Works

- *Grimus*, 1975
- *Midnight's Children*, 1981—Keskiyön lapset—*Booker-McConnell prize*
- *Shame*, 1983—Häpeä—*winner of the Prix due Meilleur Livre Étranger*
- *The Jaguar Smile: A Nicaraguan Journey*, 1987—Jaguaarin hymy: Matka Nicaraguaan
- *The Satanic Verses*, 1988—Saatanalliset Säkeet
- *Haroun and The Sea of Stories*, 1990—Harun ja Tarinoiden meri
- *In Good Faith*, 1990
- *Imaginary Homelands: Essays and Criticism*, 1991
- *Wizard of Oz*, 1992
- *East, West*, 1994—Itä, Iänsi
- *The Moor's Last Sigh*, 1995—Maurin viimeinen huokaus
- Ed.: *Mirrorwork: 50 Years of Indian Writing: 1947-1997*, 1997 (with Elisabeth West)
- *The Ground Beneath Her Feet*, 1999—Maa hänen jalkojensa alla
- *Fury, 2001*—Vimma, suom, Arto Häilä
- *Step Across This Line*, 2003
- *Shalimar, The Clown* (2005)

Although he won a certain celebrity with his second novel, the Booker prize-winning *Midnight's Children* (1981), a historical novel set at the moment that India and Pakistan achieved independence from Great Britain, it was the controversial *Satanic Verses* that made his name a household word. Its banning in India and throughout the Muslim world led to widespread demonstrations during which copies of the novel (and effigies of the author) were burnt. Rushdie was forced into hiding, moving from one safe house to another with the assistance of the British authorities and police until 1998, when Iran officially lifted the *fatwa*. The individual pieces in *East, West Stories* (1994), including the critically-celebrated, multi-voiced "Christopher Columbus and Queen Isabella of Spain Consummate Their Relationship (Santa Fe, A.D. 1992)," first published in the prestigious *New Yorker Magazine*. Dating from the same period are his children's book, *Haroun and the Sea of Stories* (1990), his book of essays, *Imaginary Homelands* (1991), and the novel *The Moor's Last Sigh* (1995).

REFERENCE

The Cambridge Biographical Dictionary, ed. Magnus Magnusson and Rosemary Goring, New York: Cambridge UP, 1990, p. 1275.

2

A Detailed Chapterwise Critical Analysis*

BOOK ONE

THE PERFORATED SHEET

The very first chapter sets the tone of comedy and satire which informs the happenings surrounding the narrator's birth and the events preceding his birth. Since his birth, Saleem, the narrator has found himself under the spell of the perforated sheet syndrome. His birth on August 15th, 1947 coincides with the birth of a new and modern nation and hence, quite mysteriously he finds himself 'handcuffed to history' and politics. His birth had been prophesied by the soothsayers and his arrival, celebrated by the politicians. Saleem will soon be thirty years old and he fears fragmentation of his over-used body. He understands that he must tell his story fast, faster than Scheherazade of the Arabian tales fame. He is after meaning and truth. He fears absurdity. He is to tell so many stories, stories of his parents and grandparents, tales of the new nation.

Saleem's story travels back in time. He tells the story of his maternal grandfather Aadam Aziz who was an educated Kashmiri Muslim and an Indian nationalist. He was exposed to western education, had spent five years in Germany to study medicine

---

*Rushdie, Salman, *Midnight's Children*. London: Vintage (1991, 1995). Further references to this text will be abbreviated *MC* and all citations are from this edition.

and returned home, a doctor. He rejected the traditional ways and beliefs in favour of modernity. His European experience bestowed upon him a scientific and rationalist world-view. Doctor Aziz returned home with a void in his head. Europe had effected a dislocation in respect of his origin and religion. His stay in Germany had altered his vision of life. One Kashmiri morning in the early spring of 1915 Aadam Aziz hit his legendary nose against the frost-hardened piece of earth while attempting to pray. Three drops of blood dropped out of his left nostril on the prayer mat. He resolved never to kiss earth for any God or man. This decision left a vacancy in his heart, and made him vulnerable to history. The years in Germany returned Aziz to a hostile home. His home-coming was looked upon as an evil intrusion into the paradisal Kashmir by the boatman Tai who represents the changeless orient. To Tai, Aziz's pigskin brief case which contained his medical instruments represented 'an alien invader, progress' (19). Tai stands for ancient India which is changeless, has a non-linear cyclical history of repetition and rebirth. He was a 'quirky, enduring familiar spirit of the valley. A watery caliban, rather too fond of cheap Kashmiri brandy' (15). He stands outside the spell of the perforated sheet spell. An overdose of brandy induces him to chatter ceaselessly. His fantastic and magical chatter used to keep Aziz spell-bound. Tai claimed to have possessed an antiquity which defied logic. He claimed to have seen Jesus Christ when he visited Kashmir. Also, he claimed to have transcended linear time and history. 'I have watched the mountains being born; I have seen emperors die' (16). Tai's view of an ageless and changeless world was lost to Dr Aziz whose western education had dispossessed him of his faith and replaced it with a firm belief in science and linear history. Tai's Kashmir stood for wholeness as against Aziz's fragmented view. It was the boatman Tai who, on the morning of Aziz's prayer time disaster in the spring of 1915, brought from the blind landowner Ghani Sahib an urgent message which set the narrative in motion. Ghani's daughter Naseem had fallen sick and the Heidelberg-returned young doctor had been called to examine the patient. The boatman Tai used to ferry the doctor to the wily landowner's house. There he was not allowed to see the patient. Naseem was a decent girl as her father exclaimed and she would not flaunt her body under the nose of the strangers. The doctor discovered an enormous white bed sheet hung in the middle of the bed chamber like a curtain and in the centre of the sheet, a hole had been cut, a crude circle about seven inches in diameter. The patient was positioned behind the perforated sheet and the doctor would examine the body of his female patient part by part through the perforated centre of the bed sheet held over her by two muscular women. The doctor-patient relationship would eventually turn into husband-wife relationship, thanks to the spell of the perforated sheet.

MERCUROCHROME

Mercurochrome is a metaphor for human blood shed due to inhuman violence inflicted on peaceful demonstrators who gathered in Jallianwala Bagh on 13 April 1919. This incident reveals the attitude of the British towards the Indians.

> Brigadier Dyer and his fifty men put down their machine-guns and go away. They fired a total of one thousand six hundred and fifty rounds into the unarmed crowed...'Good Shooting.' Dyer tells his men, 'we have done a jolly good thing' (36).

The deliberate killing of innocent people at Jallianwala Bagh did evoke protest and indignation against the colonial rule. The blood of Indians flowed on that day caused Doctor Aziz's baptism who received a severe bruise on his chest. The great Jallianwala Bagh killing took place on April 13 and a few days before, on April 6 Aziz and his newly married wife were stranded in the holy city of Amritsar on their way to Agra where he took a job as the doctor of Agra University. Padma, Saleem's female audience who gives his story the necessary ear. interferes. She is after sensation, suspense and what-happened-nextism. Saleem picks up the narrative thread and returns to the story of his grandfather which he left hanging in the air.

In those days Naseem Ghani suffered from a number of ailments and astonishingly, she did not repeat a disease. On each occasion, the young doctor was called in. She waxed anaemic in the summer and bronchial in the winter. Gradually the young doctor came to have a picture of Naseem in his mind, a collage of her severally inspected parts. The phantom of a partitioned woman began to haunt him in his dreams. Aadam Aziz had fallen under the spell of the perforated sheet much to her mother's dislike. On each occasion, the doctor was allowed a partial glimpse of the young woman's body through the medium of the perforated sheet. It was a prolonged treatment of an invisible patient which coincided with the World War I. 'Far away the Great War moved from crisis to crisis. While in the cobwebbed house of Ghani Dr Aziz was also engaged in a total war against his sectioned patient's inexhaustible complaints' (25). The doctor treats her in parts and imagines her as a whole. This synecdoche process of discovering a female body resulted in Aziz's re-integration. The Europe-returned doctor regained his mental equilibrium. Over the months and years, the young doctor did build an imaginative construction of his partitioned patient. Saleem's grandfather had fallen in love and had come to think of the perforated sheet as something magical. It was this sheet which allowed him glimpses of things which filled up the hole inside him created by his loss of religious faith. On the day in 1918 when the Great War ended, Naseem developed a bad headache and this allowed him a glimpse of his patient's face. Dr Aziz had been long waiting for the disease which gave the doctor and the patient a chance to exchange looks. Aziz's fall was complete in the garden of the earth. The wedding dowry included the perforated sheet stained with three drops of blood. When the newly wed couple left Kashmir for Agra, Aziz had the feeling of a Fall, loss of Eden. The Boatman Tai, in the meantime, had stopped cleaning his body and washing his clothes as 'gesture of unchangingness in defiance of the invasion of the doctori-attache from Heidelberg' (28). He developed a skin disease (King's Evil) of which he would be cured after Dr Aziz left the Valley. In 1918 when the Indian regiment returned from the war, Aziz's parents died in quick succession leaving him orphaned but free.

Padma, Saleem's female narratee interrupts. Saleem pleases her by a mock-serious song of praise to dung. During the stay at

Amritsar on April 6, 1919, on their way to Agra, Dr Aziz and his newly married wife Naseem came across a political agitation. It was the heyday of Gandhian nationalistic movement. A hartal (bandh) was called. It was a day of mourning, a day of protest against the infamous Rowlatt Act. Dr Aziz felt that it was his fight and he could not ignore the pull of Indian nationalism. His sense of participation in the anti-colonial protest forged his national identity. But his wife Naseem remained a decent Kashmiri girl under the veil. Aziz exhorted her to come out of *purdah* and to behave like a modern Indian woman. 'This was a struggle my grandfather never won; and it set the tone for their marriage, which rapidly developed into a place of frequent and devastating war fare' (34). The young doctor dragged all her purdah-veils and set them on fire saying, 'Forget about being a good Kashmiri girl. Start thinking about being a modern Indian woman' (34). City of Amritsar was burning. Gandhi's call for non-violence was subverted by the angry mob who invaded shops, railway stations etc. leading to the imposition of the Martial Law by the British. Dr Aziz, with his bag in hand moved around the streets bandaging the wounded, disinfecting them with mercurochrome, a medicine which looks like real human blood shed in violence. Dr Aziz did his part of a medical practitioner and contributed towards the freedom movement. This kind of active participation filled him with patriotic feelings and made him a true Indian. He embraced Indian nationalism and secular ideal. On the contrary, the boatman Tai wanted to retain his Kashmiri identity and was killed in 1947 fighting all along against Indian and Pakistani army. Narrator Saleem claims Dr Aziz as his grandparent.

HIT-THE-SPITTOON

This chapter records the components of alternative version of the official history of the partition of the country. There was before the partition, an optimism epidemic which touched Saleem's grandfather in a special sense. It was the story of one Mian Abdullah, the Hummingbird who rose from the famous Magician's ghetto in Delhi and became the hope of India's hundred million Muslims. He was the chairman and moving spirit of the Free Islam Convocation. In 1942, preparations were afoot to hold the second annual convocation of the convocation. Free Islam Convocation was for undivided India and was opposed to the idea of Pakistan as championed by the Muslim League which was believed to be a party of Muslim landowners and vested interests. Agra was a Muslim League stronghold. At the instance of the British rulers, the Leaguers murdered Mian Abdullah on the day of the convocation. Hummingbird optimists were not prepared for what happened. They played the game of hit-the-spittoon and ignored the cracks in the earth. In Agra, in the summer of 1942, Aadam Aziz like thousands of nationalist Muslims was infected by the optimism of Mian Abdullah. In those days many nationalist Muslims shared Aziz's deep-seated distrust of religious bigotry and wholeheartedly supported the Hummingbird's cause. As Aziz told Abdullah's benefactress Rani of Cooch Nahin 'I started off as a Kashmiri and not much of a Muslim. Then I got a bruise on the chest that turned me into India. I'm still not much of a Muslim, but I'm for all Abdullah. He's fighting my fight' (46).

Language of gossip, rumour and everyday talk of ordinary people, the superstitious persons at Agra pan-shops who chewed betel leaf and practised the Nawabi game of hitting the spittoon with betel juice, makes an alternative history and alternative truth. Gossip or fantasy is a subversive medium which provides the alternative view of recorded history. The official history of the freedom struggle remains silent about the embarrassment and tragedy of nationalist Muslims like Abdul Gaffar Khan of Baluchistan, popularly known as Frontier Gandhi. It only highlights the Muslim League as the sole representative of Muslims. The dreams and aspirations of those Muslims who supported a secular nation-state and rejected the partition of motherland have been 'swept under the carpet' (84). As the narrator is after truth and meaning, he depends more on gossips and rumours than on official facts ["Sometimes Legends make reality" (47).] and puts on record this unwritten episode in India's anti-colonial struggle. The narrative of the incident of the murder of Mian Abdullah, a few days before the second convocation of his party in Agra, is clothed in fantasy and grotesque. 'Six new moons came into the room, six crescent knives held by men dressed all in black, with covered faces. Two men held Nadir Khan while the others moved towards the Hummingbird' (47). The high-pitched hum of Mian Abdullah shattered the glass windows of his office. The humming sound was heard by thousands of pie-dogs who rushed to the spot of the murder and tore the murderers into pieces. Hummingbird's assistant Nadir Khan managed to escape and fled to hide in a cellar under the carpet in the house of Dr Aziz. But then Saleem, the narrator has been 'buffeted by too much history' and he fears disintegration of his body. His body is falling apart. It is this apprehension of his eventual disintegration that forces him to recollect and rewrite his history. He possesses a rare 'mastery of the multiple gifts of cookery and language' (38). During the daytime, he supervises the preparation of pickles and at night, through his nocturnal scribbling, he preserves his memory from the corruption of the clock. Whenever he appears to digress, Padma bullies him back into the world of linear narrative, her world of what-happened-next. 'At this rate,' she complains, 'you'll be two hundred years old before you manage to tell about your birth.... To me it's a crazy way of telling your life story if you can't even get to where your father met your mother' (38). Padma, Saleem's fellow-supplier of pickles and the conduit for his narrative is occasionally satisfied by periodic previews of events. Her demand for linear narrative and Saleem's need to digress pushes the narrative forward. He explains to her that he must go back two generations to tell his own story because 'the past has dripped into me.... So we can't ignore it' (38). The story leaps forward in time to 1942, the year of the Quit India movement. The narrative space moves to Agra where Saleem's grandparents had settled.

UNDER THE CARPET

At the instance of Padma, Saleem continues the thread of the narrative without any digression. Saleem is straightforward in tracing his parentage and flouts 'the halal portions of the past' (59) and, puts on record the tale of an act of privacy in his grandfather's family as well as the events of history which have been swept under the carpet. After Mia Abdullah's death, Aadam Aziz buried himself in work nursing the sick and the poor. The optimism disease was cured by the violent shock of disappointment. The gruesome killing of the Hummingbird by the fanatics put an end to the hope of a unified secular nation. Hummingbird's patron deity Rani of Cooch Nahin took to her bed. Nadir Khan, the poet who was Abdullah's lieutenant escaped murder and with the help of Rashid, a rickshaw puller, sought shelter in the basement of Aziz's house. Dr Aziz, because of his love for the idealist poet, granted him shelter in his house. This act precipitated a storm in the family. Aadam Aziz arranged to hide the optimist poet in the underground cellar of the house and thus defied his wife's objection to giving shelter to a young man in the house which was 'full of young unmarried girls' (53). The husband was determined in his resolve and Nadir Khan got asylum in the underground cell of Aziz house. In protest Naseem now called Reverend Mother stopped talking with her husband. A grim silence descended upon the house filling it 'from wall to wall, from floor to ceiling' (53) and thus leaving the inmates of the house tongue tied. But ironically in that 'bog of muteness' (54) in the Aziz house where 'life had been transmuted into grotesquery by the irruption into it of history' (57), a dream of love and romance unfolded itself.

Major Zulfikar, a military man, an army officer visited Dr Aziz's house in connection with the enquiry of the murder of Mia Abdullah. There he saw Emerald, the youngest daughter of Dr Aziz and fell in love with her. Emerald, the most beautiful of the three Aziz daughters was also the most precocious of the three. She was not yet fifteen but possessed an adult gaze in her eyes. She realized that this unattractive army officer was a promising man and agreed to marry him despite his clumsy appearance. Alia, the eldest of the sisters was the most brilliant. She was of twenty-one years and read at the University. She was wooed by a young leather-cloth merchant, Ahmed Sinai who had been divorced at twenty. He met Alia at the University and was impressed by the manners of this grave and bookish girl. But he did not find an opportune moment to propose to Alia and ask for her hand because the death-like silence in Aziz household made him unnerved. The nineteen years old second daughter of the Aziz house, Mumtaz, whom her mother could not love because of her dark complexion, was neither intelligent like Alia nor beautiful like Emerald. She was dark but deep; she was a nice girl, decent in demeanour, good and lonely. She loved her father Cordelia like. She knew that an old man requires care and affection. This dark and unassuming daughter, Mumtaz caught the fancy of Ahmed Sinai who was after love from a tender soul and desired children as his earlier wife could not give him any. In other words, Mumtaz also fell in love with Ahmed Sinai in no time. It was an unexpressed love.

Nadir Khan, the rhymeless poet who fled from the assassins and sought shelter in Dr Aziz's house and which was immediately granted by the Doctor, hid in the half-lit underworld of Aziz house. Mumtaz the loving girl took upon herself the task of looking after the guest under the carpet. Everyday she descended into the underground cellar to carry his food and do other useful things. There in the darkness of the cellar she was wooed and courted by the rhymeless bard. Nadir Khan asked Dr Aziz for his daughter's hand and in the summer of 1943 Mumtaz married Nadir in a secret ceremony which was attended by the family members except the mother who had chosen to remain immured in her room with her web of silence (57). After her marriage, Mumtaz started living a double wife, one in public and other, private. During day-time she was a single girl living with her parents and studying at the University. At night she descended into her marriage chamber which her poet-husband fancifully called Taj Mahal. There in the lamp-lit seclusion of the Taj, the couple played an ancient game with a silver spittoon which the dying Rani of Cooch Nahin sent them as a wedding gift. On the other hand, the Reverend Mother began to swell quite comically under the pressure of unspoken words. Enough materials of tragedy and comedy got being stored in the events all around. In August 1945, Saleem's benefactress Rani of Cooch Nahin died amid rains. Subhas Chandra Bose's INA fought a pitched battle with the British soldiers in the rain-soaked forests of Burma while the Satyagrahis in India were staging non-violent demonstration against the British rulers. Mumtaz fell seriously ill in her underground cellar. A physical check-up by the doctor father tragically revealed that the marriage of his daughter, in spite of two-year long stay with Nadir Khan, remained unconsummated. To speak comically, the impotent idealist had failed to hit her spittoon and redeem his promise. This shocking revelation led to an outburst from the Reverend Mother whose pent-up words burst in a storm and hit her embarrassed husband. She continued pouring out her long suppressed grievances against her husband whom she held responsible for the sorry plight of her dark daughter. Emerald ran to Major Zulfikar unveiled and divulged the carefully guarded family secret. On that very day, August 9, 1945, America dropped an unheard-of weapon on the cities of Japan and at home, Emerald used her weapon against the 'fountainhead of family's troubles' (61) and revealed the secret of underground cellar to Zulfikar who rushed to Aziz house to apprehend the suspect in the Abdullah murder case. But Nadir Khan successfully eluded Zulfikar and his soldiers and left a message of divorce. In January 1946 Major Zulfikar married Emerald, the youngest and shrewd daughter of Dr Aziz after the storm in the family subsided. And now was the time when once divorced Ahmed Sinai discovered in the newly divorced Mumtaz a kindred soul. Alia remained silent following Mumtaz, her younger sister stealing her fiancé. In June that year, Mumtaz remarried. Ahmed Sinai, her new husband gave her a new name Amina. The newly married couple started for Delhi to re-build a new house there, leaving behind a sad and embittered Amina for whom it was the 'unkindest cut'. She felt 'bruised ever more badly than her father in Jallianwalabag' (94).

A PUBLIC ANNOUNCEMENT

Mumtaz's unproductive years with Nadir Khan in the underground cellar became a thing of the past and she resurfaced in Delhi in the new name of Amina Sinai, wife of Ahmed Sinai and official (not biological) mother of Saleem Sinai. Political atmosphere of pre-partition Delhi in January 1947 was charged with communal hatred and violence. The events were moving fast towards the inevitable end of the colonial rule and the birth of a nation. The Cabinet Mission scheme for the transfer of power failed and paved the way for the last Viceroy, Earl

Mountbatten who would appear in the political firmament with his Soldier's Knife and would cut the subcontinent into two and subsequently three parts. In this situation of political and communal turmoil, Amina reached Old Delhi with her husband to settle down to a new life. The story digresses. But then Padma gets irritated whenever Saleem's narration becomes self-conscious. Also she was alarmed at Saleem's mention of cracks and fissures in his body. She called in a quack to examine him but the doctor declared him 'whole' and cast doubt on the stability of his mind and thus on his reliability as a narrator. The doctor found no crack in Saleem's body. However, Padma is pacified and Saleem takes up the narrative thread and describes Amina's new life, her role as Ahmed Sinai's wife. With her natural gifts of assiduity, care and love, she transformed the orphan's dwelling (Ahmed Sinai became early in life an orphan) into 'something gentle and loving' (67). She showed her mettle by winning the heart of her new husband. Her personal struggle with her old self proved formidable as her mind was still clogged up with the memory of the first man in her life, Nadir Khan. The rhymeless bard visited her in dream and it prevented her from giving her husband unquestioned devotion. However, she was undaunted in her resolve. She began an experiment of loving her husband part by part everyday. In the process, she fell a victim to the legacy of her father, the spell of the perforated sheet and fragmentation syndrome. As a result, she was unable to love her husband in full, she learned to love the different parts of her husband separately, to love him in segments. 'She resolved to fall in love with her husband bit by bit' (68). Amina accepted and loved her husband in fragments and then, in whole Ahmed Sinai came to resemble for Amina 'a man he had never known and an underground chamber he had never seen' (68-69). In her private world Amina was struggling and trying to overcome the fragmentation disease and saw her husband 'whole.' In contrast, the political and geographical space of the country, in those times, was going into fragments. Dream of Dr Aziz and many other nationalist optimists for a unified and secular India was shattered into pieces in the wake of the rise of pre-partition violence and religious fanaticism.

Ahmed Sinai was doing well in his leather-cloth business and shared his go-down with two other Muslim businessmen, Mustapha Kamal and S.P. Butt at the industrial estate on the outskirts of Old Delhi. Time was out of joint. Ahmed's estate was put on fire by the religious fundamentalists. On a January morning in 1947, Ahmed got the information of arson from his co-businessmen and all the three in a panic left for their warehouse. At his dear home, Amina was getting ready to reveal the secret of her pregnancy to her husband. Communal frenzy outside denied her the bliss. It was a bad time when a fanatical Hindu revivalist group named the Ravana gang terrorized and blackmailed Muslim businessmen and burnt down their shops and factories if they failed to give in time the protection money. They were not satisfied with Ahmed Sinai and hence misfortune visited the Sinai family. Ahmed left the house leaving Amina behind with her undisclosed secret.

That very moment, in that Muslim neighbourhood, there appeared a peep-show man named Lifafa Das. He was a Hindu youth with a smile. He used to visit the Muslim mahalla with his mobile 'Dunia dekho' machine. Because of the magical rattle of his 'dugdugee' he attracted children and also the adults into the street and showed them the collage of an India that was a 'whole,' a unified India. 'Inside the peep show were pictures of the Taj Mahal and Meenakshi Temple, and the holy Ganges...' (75). Perhaps, Lifafa Das, like Nadir Khan, the dreamer, suffered from an Indian urge 'to encapsulate the whole of reality' (75). He stuffed his magic box with many pictures to make good his promise to the people to show them the whole world. He stood for unity and harmony. It was a worst morning when a small quarrel among the children about who would put his eyes first at the hole in the peep-show box turned communal. The violent Muslim crowd jumped and gheraoed the lone Hindu. Dr Aziz's daughter Mumtaj turned Amina witnessed the public frenzy from her doors and rushed to the rescue of Lifafa Das. Did not she possess the parental gift of religious tolerance and hatred for religious prejudice? Her only weapon was the public announcement of her pregnancy even before her husband had heard about it. 'Listen well, I'm with child. I am a mother who will have a child, and I am giving this man my shelter. Come on now, if you want to kill, kill a mother and show the world what men you are!' (77). This was an announcement of Saleem's arrival, and which turned him into 'public property' (77) much before his birth. The spectacle of Amina's motherhood (full womb) before the frenzied crowd presented an image of unity and wholeness and saved Lifafa's life. The grateful youth reciprocated Amina's graceful gesture by offering the gift of a prophecy about her unborn child.

MANY-HEADED MONSTERS

Saleem reconstructs incidents in history and in private life from many generations prior to his birth and acknowledges the intervention of chance in the chain of causality. 'A filmy curtain of ambiguities' (87) he observes, pervades the events in history and even in the life of an individual. He believes in a kind of fatalism. 'My mother's pregnancy, it seems, was fated; my birth, however, owed a good deal to accident' (79). Saleem reflects on the relationship between 'birth' and 'reality.' 'Truth' he observes, lies hidden inside the narrative. His story offers a fictional alternative to the linear historical narrative.

This chapter narrates two parallel episodes; Amina Sinai's visit to the fortune-teller Ramram Seth accompanied with Lifafa Das and, Ahmed Sinai's difficult and unpleasant encounter with the fanatical monsters. Amina Sinai had been waiting for a suitable moment to accept Lifafa Das's offer of visiting the fortune-teller, but for two days after the burning of his factory, Ahmed Sinai stayed at home. He was getting ready for the unpleasant encounter. Five minutes after he left for the Old Fort with his grey moneybag which contained the protection money, Amina Sinai set off for the Red Fort, for her secret adventure. Both the journeys had far-reaching consequences: 'one foretold future; the other settled its geographical location' (80). At the end of both the roads, there lay many-headed monsters, representing in the case of Ahmed Sinai, the fanatical anti-Muslim Ravana-gang and, in the case of Amina Sinai, Saleem's monstrous suspicion about the truth of the prophecy about him. 'Suspicion is a monster with many heads' (88). Both husband

and wife made a journey to the Old Fort and Red Fort respectively but with different results. Amina was blessed with the prophecy of the birth of a son while Ahmed Sinai's journey resulted in a disaster. Many headed monster of communalism raised its ugly head. There were anonymous phone calls from the Muslim hating fanatics and Ahmed Sinai along with two other fellow businessmen, Kemal and Butt reached the destination, the ruins of the Old Fort, each carrying under the coat a grey bag full of money. It is to this ruin of an antique time that Kemal, Butt and Ahmed Sinai had been brought by an anonymous phone call. Ahmed left his bag in the turret of the crumbling fort and began to wait in its shadow. He was terribly worried. His was an unfulfilled ambition of re-arranging 'the Quran in accurately chronological order' (82). He was also tormented with the thought of the future geographical location of his estate. He was to choose between the offer of Major Zulfikar who advised him to go to the new state of Pakistan when it would come up and the offer of his friend Doctor Narlikar who requested him to shift his property to Bombay. His reverie was cut short by the shadowy appearance of the monster from the shadow of his ruined room, the appointed representative of the Ravana gang. But before the demon could collect the booty, a strange incident took place. An enraged monkey by way of protesting the intrusion of humans in his territory, pounced on the moneybags, tore them and threw the bundles of currency notes down into the ditch. The panicky businessmen could hear the threats of revenge from the demonic money collector and were dismayed at the cruel joke of the circumstances.

While the panic-stricken businessmen were engaged in picking up rupees from the pools of urine and rotting fruits, Amina was on her way to Ramram Seth. She took her journey in a taxi. Lifafa Das was her guide to her destination. The taxi moved through the narrow, crowded streets of Old Delhi where people led their 'invisible lives' like some terrible monster with many heads. She climbed the dark stairs and at last saw the soothsayer Ramram Seth sitting cross legged, six inches above the ground. He was surrounded by monkeys, snakes and vultures. Amina screamed but soon received the oracular predictions about her child from the strange fortune-teller, 'history speaking through his lips' (87). Ramram predicted a son,

> A son, Sahiba, who will never be older than his motherland—neither older nor younger.... There will be two heads but you will see only one—there will be knees and a nose, a nose and knees.... Newspaper praises him, two mothers raise him!... Washing will hide him—Voices will guide him! Spittoons will brain him—doctors will drain him—Soldiers will try him—tyrants will fry him.... He will have sons without having sons!... And he will die before he is dead (87-88).

Ramram's prophecy carries an equivocal meaning *vis-à-vis* the birth of Amina's son. This prophecy foreshadows future events that will take place in the lives of the children born at midnight hours. Saleem's suspicion regarding the authenticity of the prophecy torments him. Suspicion is, of course, a many-headed monster.

Ahmed Sinai returned home that gruesome night from the ruins of his gutted factory. He decided to leave Delhi and move to Bombay to invest in real estate. On 4th June 1947, Mountbatten held a press conference and announced the partition of the subcontinent. Saleem's 'ill-matched parents' pushed by many-headed monsters left for Bombay. The countdown for the fulfilment of the ambiguous prophecy started.

METHWOLD

In the city of Old Delhi, Amina Sinai made her public announcement and now the story shifts to the metropolitan city of Bombay, the city of Saleem's birth. Saleem loves the city of Bombay and feels nostalgic. As a matter of fact *Midnight's Children* is a city novel and Bombay of 1950s is the fictive space. Events of almost half the book take place here in this sprawling city. The cosmopolitan city of 1950s Bombay with its composite and secular culture stands as a metaphor for the plurality and multiplicity of India. Bombay remains the central metaphor which informs this vast novel of epic dimension. This ancient city of seven islands is brought alive through the description of historical details, myths and legends.

'Our Bombay, Padma! It was very different then' (106). Saleem identifies himself with the historical city of Bombay, the city of Mumbadevi, reclaimed by the foreigners. The Portuguese named the place Bom-Bahia for its harbour. Mumbadevi, in course of time has been replaced by elephant-headed Ganesh. The chief festival is Ganesh Chaturthi when big processions are taken out. The narrator regretfully describes how this ancient city was colonized by the successive invaders from the Portuguese to the British. And now the British were about to depart themselves in August 1947.

Saleem's parents came in this city in June 19 two months before the end of British dominion and entered into a curious bargain with one such departing Englishman. His name was William Methwold. Methwold decided to sell his property at a low price before returning home. He was a tall man with a prominent nose and centrally parted hair and he claimed descendence from an officer of the East India Company. He accepted the turn in history which declared the end of the Raj with a bit of salt. Transfer of power was an inevitable fact and he could read the writing on the wall. 'I'm dead against it myself, but what's to be done' (96). As a Briton who stood for moral depravity of the British colonization, Methwold played an imperialistic game by dramatizing his 'transfer of assets.' His bargain with Ahmed Sinai exposes the sinister colonial game the British had played since Macaulay's time. Ahmed Sinai and the persons like him who were Indian by birth but English at heart were the suitable customers who would inherit the mantle of power and would step into the departing colonialists' shoes. Methwold's Estate symbolizes the colonized India, possessed by the British who had superimposed their culture on Indian mind. Thus the 'transfer of assets' has a special connotation. It is a parody of the transfer of power. 'My notion is to stage my transfer of assets. Select suitable persons—such as yourself, Mr Sinai!—hand everything over absolutely intact: in tip-top working order' (111). Methwold's Estate consisting of four identical houses built in European style and named after royal palaces in Europe was sold to select members of Indian elite and that too, on two conditions. The houses should be bought with every item in them and the entire contents were to be retained by the new owners and that the 'actual transfer should not take place until midnight on August 15' (95). The passage amply reflects on the myth of the empire. 'You'll admit we weren't all bad: built your roads, schools, railways, parliamentary system, all worthwhile things' (96) Methwold tells Ahmed Sinai. Transfer of power suggests perpetuation of colonial system. It means the passing on of the mantle to the Indian elite who inherited political power from the colonial masters and aped the airs of the masters. Ahmed Sinai who speaks in oxford drawl, perhaps resembles Jawaharlal Nehru. Post-colonial reality is a glaring example of the fact that the transfer of power on Indian political class does not make us free from psychological slavery of the west. It is a kind of freedom for the rich and the privileged. The poor and the dispossessed have nothing to gain except poverty, squalor and their involvement in fratricide to make the freedom for the rich a reality. Now who were the chosen heirs of the Methwold Estate? They were the Sinais, Homi Catrack, the Ibrahims, Dr Narlikar and Sabarmati and his wife Lila. They found themselves gradually changing into an indigenous elite class by the 'subtle magic' of the place. They adapted themselves to the life-style of the colonial masters. Their myth-world stood in sharp contrast to the space of the poverty-stricken millions of their countrymen. Amina Sinai was the only inhabitant of the Methwold Estate who could not identify herself with the glare of the myth world. She felt that the 'tick-tock of count down calendars was rushing everyone towards August 15th' (101). The Bombay edition of the *Times of India* announced that it would award a prize to any Bombay mother who could arrange to give birth to a child at the precise moment of the birth of a new nation. Amina was certain that she would win the prize. There were other pregnant women around. Vanita, wife of the street musician Willie Winkie, was pregnant and her pregnancy was the result of Methwold's guilt.

Mary Pereira was a midwife at Narlikar's nursing home. She hated the rich at the instance of her communist mentor Joseph who was enraged at the partition riots and observed, 'This independence is for the rich only and the poor are made to kill each other like flies' (103). Mary decided to commit a crime on the night of 15 August and thus to make 'important contribution to the history of twentieth century' (104). Saleem's birth being the dividing line between the old world and the new, the chapter ends with a countdown to 'inevitable midnight' (106).

TICK, TOCK

Padma also could hear the countdown to an inevitable midnight. She is after suspense and what happens next. 'There is nothing like a countdown for building suspense' (106). Saleem promised that he would tell the story of his birth but that he was under necessity to make a summary of past events. It was memory's past. In his memory, past and present co-existed. He was given the power or magical skill to report events that took place in his pre-natal past, events that were connected with the history of the country. The events of the past constituted his inheritance. Lives of people and events that took place in the past were interwined. Saleem's inheritance included the lives and events like the loss of faith of Aadam Aziz, his oath, not to bow down before God or man, the hole in his heart which was filled by a woman behind the perforated sheet. Years ticking away and his inheritance grew to include the mythical teeth of the boatman Tai and his brandy bottle and then Mahatma Gandhi and his hartal. His inheritance also included the gift of inventing new parents for himself whenever necessary. Innumerable events and lives to the moment of independence had been Saleem's inheritance, 'part of the luggage brought into the world' (108). They were 'the parents of the child born on that midnight' (108). Saleem is the swallower of lives innumerable. 'To understand just one life, you have to swallow the world' (109). This inclusive style of narrating which contains 'wild profusion' of events thrives on multiple levels of meaning. Distinctions between fact and fiction, individual and world are simply wished away.

Midnight's Children is related to the history, country and the world and thus remains an Indian work of art which is pluralistic despite its inheritance from the western novel genre. The narrator-protagonist is a grotesque character but is endowed with omniscience. Multiplicity of events has been woven into his life as well as his narrative. 'If I seem a little bizarre, remember the wild profusion of my inheritance...perhaps if one wishes to remain an individual in the midst of the teeming multitudes, one must make oneself grotesque' (109). Padma is satisfied as she understands that at last Saleem learned how to tell things really fast.

Reporting of subsequent events has been elaborately done. Events leading to the simultaneous birth of the nation (India) and its body (Saleem) between August 13 and 15 are reported in a colourful way. Unceasing countdown to the inevitable moment (tick, tock) wonderfully captures the euphoria and tension of independence. The frantic representations of the astrologers to the Congress party bosses, the 'mass blood-letting' (112) on the frontiers of the divided Punjab, communal violence, Gandhi's peace march in Bengal etc. constitute the items of public drama; while private rituals of Amina Sinai and Vanita keep pace. On 14th August, Vanita, the wife of Wee Willie Winkie—entered into a prolonged, unproductive labour in the charity ward of Dr Narlikar's Nursing Home. The first pangs hit her when, 'hundreds of miles away, M.A. Jinnah announced the midnight birth of a Muslim nation' (111). On the other side of the border, there were rituals of blood to celebrate the birth of a 'new myth,' the myth of a nation that is India. Saleem writes,

> ...a nation which had never previously existed was about to win its freedom, catapulting us into a world which, although it had five thousand years of history ...was nevertheless quite imaginary, into a mythical land, a country which would never exist except by the efforts of a phenomenal collective will—except in a dream we all agreed to dream (112).

And six hours before midnight on August 15 William Methwold finally transferred his property to his Indian heirs and left the country for good. But he left his deception behind in the womb of poor Vanita who writhed on a bed in the charity ward. One could hear the shrieks of a woman in labour, but the baby showed no sign of coming nor its father present. At the same hour Amina went into a 'prophecy-ridden' labour in a cabin of the Narlikar Nursing Home. Saleem's arrival into independent India coincides with Nehru's promise of a secular country. The hour of independence is projected through celebrations and rituals in the streets and, in Bombay, August is the month of festivals. National tri-colour flag is unfurled and the Prime Minister Nehru makes his eloquent speech in the Assembly Hall in Delhi. In between these officially recorded events, are the labour pains of expecting mothers, partition riots, fires and the acts of violence. Unilinear version of the history of the independence is replaced by the montage which represents the multiple vision of alternative reality. Just at the midnight hour when twin children were born, one to Amina and other to Vanita; the midwife Mary Pereira, out of her own sense of revenge, committed a 'private revolutionary act' (117). She changed the name tags of the babies "giving the poor baby a life of privilege and condemning the rich born child to poverty" (117). Saleem, actually poor Vanita's child found Amina as her mother and became 'the chosen child of midnight' to win the *Times of India* prize and receive Prime Minister Nehru's letter of congratulation. In reality he was an Anglo Indian, the illegitimate son of a departing colonizer and a poor Hindu woman. If Saleem represents the newly born post-colonial nation-state, then the matter of illegitimacy informs the birth of the post-colonial country which is also the product of time and history. 'In fact, all over the new India, the dream we all shared, children were being born who were only partially the offspring of their parents—the children of midnight were also the children of the time: fathered, you understand by history' (118). Post-colonial children have nothing to do with the concept of origin or purity. Time is hybrid and so is history. There are curves in the movement of time and of history. When the Sinais eventually discovered the betrayal of Mary Pereira, they reconciled themselves to the fact of Saleem's miscegenation.

'We all found that it made no difference! I was still their son: they remained my parents. In a kind of collective failure of imagination we learned that we simply could not think our way out of our pasts' (118).

BOOK TWO

Book two records the growth and development of Saleem from childhood to adolescence. The period of his attaining adulthood is fraught with the uncanny feeling of fragmentation. Saleem's fragmented selfhood mirrors the growth and development of the nation between 1947 and 1965. The newly independent nation shows cracks and fissures in its polity as the major historical events illustrate. Some of these events are, the assassination of Mahatma Gandhi, India's five-year plans, the linguistic reorganization of Indian states and consequent language riots, the imposition of Martial Law in Pakistan in 1958, the Chinese aggression in 1962, the theft of the sacred relic from Hazratbal Mosque in Srinagar, Nehru's death and the Indo-Pakistan war in 1965. At the family level, this section traces the fortunes of Saleem's parents and near relations, the migration of the Sinais to Pakistan and their destruction in the war of 1965. The enthusiasm generated at the moment of freedom on August 15 was rapidly on the wane. There was widespread disillusionment resulting from corruption at high places and the failure of the successive Governments to live up to the promise as the first Prime Minister in the Assembly Hall at the midnight hour, proclaimed in his speech. The gradual disintegration of Saleem's body is metaphorically combined with the cracking up of the nation.

THE FISHERMAN'S POINTING FINGER

The story of Saleem's flawed genealogy was distasteful to his listener Padma and, even to average readers. The framing of his fragmented self with the tools of memory is a reflection on Saleem's fractured vision of history and nation. The fragmentation of self has been the legacy of his grandfather Aadam Aziz, 'Condemned by a perforated sheet to a life of fragments,' Saleem comments. But then Aadam Aziz was the victim of the perforated sheet but Saleem became the master, because of his narrative skill. And now Padma, the narratee found herself under the spell of the perforated sheet and so, are the audience of this comic drama of soul. Padma has been, as Saleem comments, 'captivated by love' (121). Padma favours linear narrative and not digression. Hence she expresses her rage at the mention of the word 'love' by an impotent narrator whose writing is a substitute for 'other pencil.' She is disgusted with this writing business, calls Saleem a mad man and departs from his narrative. Thus abandoned, Saleem returns to his work.

Padma's accusing finger reminds Saleem of a fisherman's pointing finger. There is a picture of the fisherman, Tai pointing his finger to the western horizon, hung on the wall of baby Saleem's bedroom in Buckingham Villa in the Methwold Estate. This pointing finger of the boatman continuously reminds him of the oriental vision of wholeness as against fragments. Saleem or, for that matter, the newly born nation is condemned to a life of fragmentation and hence, Saleem, at birth, is handcuffed to history. The pointing finger is prophetic as it points out the 'special doom' and 'inescapable destiny' which awaits Saleem the narrator and the newly born nation.

Baby Saleem and also the new nation started their respective journey with optimism and confidence since their moment of birth. Saleem's central position was ratified by the prime minister and his photograph appeared on the front page of the *Times of India*.

> Newspapers celebrated me: politicians ratified my position. Jawaharlal Nehru wrote: Dear Baby Saleem, My belated congratulations on the happy accident of your moment of birth! You are the newest bearer of that ancient face of India which is also eternally young. We shall be watching over your life with the closest attention; it will be, in a sense, the mirror of our own (122).

Thus after being assured of his central role as the mirror of the nation, baby Saleem arrived home from the nursing home with his umbilical chord preserved in a pickle jar. Thereafter, he embarked on a 'heroic programme of self-enlargement' (124) under the eyes of his twin mothers. The event of his huge appetite and fantastic growth is comically and metaphorically combined with India's ambitious five-year plans and the huge amount of foreign aid these five-year plans devoured. Saleem's grotesque figure represents the map of India which got disfigured because of the partition of its geography. This child of midnight was born with magical power and was liked and favoured by the inhabitants of the Methwold Estate. As a matter of fact, Saleem found his place 'at the centre of the universe' (126). Another child of midnight, Shiva continues visiting the Methold Estate with his poor father Willie Winkie, now a widower and a victim of throat cancer. As the poor minstrel entertained the inhabitants of Methwold Estate with his song of sadness, his son Shiva with knees sat at his feet and was filled with unspeakable rage. Shiva is the Puranic God of procreation and destruction. Only Mary's crime deprived him of his birthright and he was doomed to a life of poverty. He would descend to Bombay's underworld and stand antagonistic to Saleem's centrality. The antagonism between Saleem's search for meaning and Shiva's propensity to chaos constitutes the focal point of the narrative. Saleem stands for order and elitism while Shiva, for violence. Together, they constitute the contradictory forces of Indian political system. Saleem's position exerted an influence on history and on the lives of the individuals including the life of his father Ahmed Sinai. 'I lay in my crib and listened; and everything that happened, happened because of me' (133). Saleem felt himself responsible for both private and public lives. Thus he stands as a polar opposite to Shiva who represents the 'other', the mindless mob, violence and anarchy.

SNAKES AND LADDERS

The game of snakes and ladders refers to the fluctuating fortunes of the Sinai family. In those days Ahmed Sinai invested huge sums of money in different projects and amassed fabulous wealth. This led to the freezing of his assets. The subcontinent was partitioned on the basis of religion. After the partition, the Government of India ordered the freezing of the assets of many Muslim businessmen and Ahmed Sinai's assets were also illegally frozen. This blow of fortune had been too hard for Ahmed to bear and he fell ill and was bed-ridden. He was as cold as ice. The title of the chapter metaphorically states that one falls but to rise and that the snakebite pulls a man down while the ladder lifts him up. It was the worst of time but also the best. At the dramatic reversal of the fortunes of Sinai family, Amina's womanly dedication 'rose to new heights' (136). There followed good fortune for the family and a warmth in the conjugal life. Saleem's sister, Brass Monkey was born.

It was the winter of 1948 and Ahmed Sinai experienced a winter in his life due to the freezing of his assets by the government. The threat of penury and pain unnerved him. At that time when the family fortune was at the low ebb, a European snake expert visited the Methwold Estate. He was allowed to stay in the upper storey of Buckingham Villa on rent. This man was a scientist who did research work on snake poison for medicinal purposes. So snakes and ladders appropriately explain the state of the Goddess of the family fortune. It is said, Goddess of fortune (Lakshmi) is fickle. It was the time when the Lakshmi left the Sinais. Amina wrote to her parents to come to her rescue. Dr Aziz and Naseem arrived at Methwold Estate and stood by the Sinai family in the hour of crisis. Reverend mother told Amina, her daughter, that she (Naseem) would run the kitchen and prepare food for Ahmed so that he might go strong again. Dr Aziz examined his son-in-law and Reverend mother announced, 'This is no time to hide in bed. Now he must be a man and do a man's business' (139). Ahmed Sinai stayed in bed and moaned from time to time. 'Smashed, wife! Snapped—like an icicle' (140). Amina was freed from the exigencies of running her home. She decided to put things right by her own effort. She went to gamble in the race course. As the narrator comments, 'With the Brass Monkey growing inside her, my mother stalked the paddocks of the race course named after the Goddess of Wealth, braving early morning sickness' (142). She was ignorant of the first thing about horses and the rules of the race but she won with surprising regularity. And now the Goddess of Fortune smiled on her. With the Money won in the races, she fought a legal battle against the government and won the case. Ahmed Sinai got back his assets by the order of the High Court.

All games have morals. The game of snakes and ladders preaches the commonplace truth that every ladder you climb, a snake is waiting just around the corner and for every snake, a ladder will compensate. That evening, Amina went to the premiere of Hanif's (her brother) first feature film 'The Lovers of Kashmir' along with her husband. This film was starred by Hanif's wife Pia. While they were watching Hanif's technique of 'indirect kiss,' an enjoyable parody of Bombay cinema's prudery during the '50s, a revolutionary technique which would help him climb the ladder; a terrible announcement by the hall manager brought the show to an abrupt end. The announcement was short but fraught with far-reaching consequences. 'This afternoon, at Birla House in Delhi, our beloved Mahatma was killed. Some madman shot him in the stomach, ladies and gentlemen—our Bapu is gone!' (143). The snake of religious fanaticism raised its ugly head just at the moment when Hanif was about to climb the ladder of success. There was an abortive end of the film. For forty-eight hours, the family remained confined within the walls of Buckingham Villa till there was a radio announcement that one Hindu fanatic killed the Mahatma. For every ladder, there is a snake.

The race course ended. There was a theft in the Sinai household. Mary, the Christian nurse was proud of her superior status in the family and quarreled with Musa, the Muslim servant. Among other things, the silver spittoon, a marriage gift to the Sinais from the Rani of Cooch Nahin was stolen and it was found in the bedroll of Musa. The police search took place. The police search continued in the Methwold Estate and one Joseph, Mary Pereira's mentor and who was on the most wanted list of the police was shot at. He was supposedly involved in the making of explosive bombs. Life at the Buckingham Villa turned melodramatic, melodrama piling upon melodrama, assuming the colour of a Bombay talkie. Baby Saleem fell ill; he developed typhoid. Dr Aziz felt helpless and declared that the boy would be dead in no time. At that crucial moment, the European snake charmer handed Dr Aziz a little bottle. It was the medicine prepared out of the venom of king cobra. Only two drops would cure the boy. And so it did. Baby Saleem was administered poison which spread through the child's body and six hours later, his temperature had returned to normal. There is the other version of the puzzle *Snakes and Ladders*. Snakes can lead to cure and victory and ladders are not always for ascending but can be descended too. Life is an ambiguity, an unsolvable puzzle.

ACCIDENT IN A WASHING-CHEST

Padma walked out on him halfway and Saleem felt lonely and abandoned. A balance had been upset. Padma's ignorance and superstition worked as counterweights to his miracle-laden omniscience. Saleem felt cracks widening down the length of his body. He was without the necessary ear. At the age of nine, Saleem was obsessed with the idea that he was born to do great things. He was troubled with the thought of purpose or meaning of existence. He began to be haunted by the fear 'that my much trumpeted existence might turn out to be utterly useless, void, and without any shred of a purpose' (152). He found himself surrounded by people who seemed to possess a sense of purpose of their lives. His friends or schoolmates had their aim in life or future goal. Only Saleem was not sure of his purpose. He was anxious to know the meaning of existence. He was under the terrible notion that he, alone in the universe, had no idea of what he should be or how he should behave. To get rid of this nagging sense of purposelessness, Saleem buried himself in fairly-tales and comic books. He imagined himself in the role of Aladin, voyaging in a fabulous cave. Hatim Tai and Batman, Superman and Sindbad moved his fancy. It was a very early age at which one is perplexed by meaning and purpose of life.

His sister Brass Monkey was as beautiful as he was ugly. She was as mischievous as a whirlwind and noisy as a crowd. Saleem treated her as an ally, not a competitor and she never blamed him for his pre-eminence in the house. In his ninth year, Saleem was sent to school but his experience at school was not happy either. On his first day at school, Miss Kapadia, the teacher who had turned from her blackboard to greet him, saw his long nose, and dropped her duster in alarm, smashing the nail on her big toe. Saleem was once again ashamed of his ugliness.

He knew this much that everybody was waiting for him. Prophets and prime ministers had created around him a halo of expectancy. His father expected him to do great things. To escape from the demands of real life, Saleem started hiding in his mother's large white washing chest which provided him with a shelter from the pressures of reality. Real world was too much for him. In his hiding place he felt safe from all pressures of life and burdens of time. He could forget the conquest of the Mount Everest, the Suez Crisis and the Five Year Plans. In the safety of the washing chest, Saleem felt the safety of the womb. It was from his hiding place that he discovered his mother's duplicity. It was an accident. It was a revelation. During the summer of that year, Amina, wife of Ahmed Sinai, used to receive a series of telephone calls. Brass Monkey answered one such telephone call in her absence. She heard, on the other side, the soft, fleshy voice of a poet. There developed a suspicion in Saleem's mind that his mother might have a secret. The suspicion turned into reality by an event a few days later. From his hiding in the washing chest, Saleem heard his mother answering a telephone call. Then she came to the privacy of her bathroom and cried while uttering a long forgotten name, Nadir Khan. His mother's perfidy was to Saleem, a revelation which coincided with an accident. A pajama chord somehow got inserted into his left nostril and caused a violent sniff. This event bestowed on him the power of telepathy. It happened so comically and fantastically. Saleem lost his hiding. He was banished from the washing chest by his guilt-ridden mother but his gain was great, the mantle of greatness settling upon his shoulders. Now he could hear voices, 'Like Musa or Moses, like Muhammad the Penultimate, I heard voices on a hill' (163). He discovered that he was a radio receiver and could select individual voices. He could even switch off his newly discovered inner ear.

Saleem disclosed the sublime gift of his revelation to the unbelieving family members next morning but nobody took him seriously. His mother thought that he was mad. His irate father gave a mighty blow on the side of his head that made him permanently deaf in the left ear. For the rest of his life, Saleem was plagued by constant doubts about what he was for. That night, Amina Sinai dreamt of the soothsayer Ramram Seth and his prediction 'Washing will hide him...voices will guide him' (165).

ALL INDIA RADIO

Saleem did develop his inner air. He did hear voices. His head had become All India Radio which could receive voices. But he is afraid of his parent's wrath and keeps his knowledge a secret. At midnight, he wakes up from sleep and tunes his inner ear to disembodied voices which were not sacred but profane. He hears telepathically the 'inner monologues of all the teeming millions of masses and classes alike' (168). He describes the language riot that rocked Bombay in 1956. Language divides Indians in postcolonial times. Saleem's miraculous power is at work. 'The voices babbled in everything from Malayalam to Naga dialects, from the purity of Lucknow Urdu to the southern slurring of Tamil' (168). Saleem's narrative now comes nearer the events of the present and becomes episodic and fragmentary. Padma's absence has only created confusion and uncertainties. His memory plays tricks with him. He discovers that he has made a chronological error in dating the assassination of Mahatma Gandhi. This proves that Saleem is an unreliable narrator and that he is capable of distortion and error. He is not a sure guide and chronicler. The reader is asked to make his/her own judgment. This is more so because in his desperate bid for meaning and purpose he rewrites the whole history of his time in order to empower the children of the midnight to place him in a central role. He does not believe in the literal facts of history. He is rewriting the history of India, a country which itself is a dream. 'In my India, Gandhi will continue to die at the wrong time' (166). The child narrator who is of nine years of age and is lost in the confusion of other people's lives. Both the child narrator and the child nation suffered from 'confused thinking'. In order to seek refuge from his inner turmoil, Saleem retreated into the empty clock tower and from the privacy of the broken down clock tower he saw the great events happening around. Saleem began a psychic journey through the length and breadth of the country its geography and could know its politics and economics. At this point, the child narrator's narrative becomes an indictment of the child nation's society and values. The politics and economics of the new nation are found to be characterized by exploitation, corruption at all levels, bribery and electoral malpractices. The telepathic power of 'mind hopping' gave him the illusion of an artist. He entered the mind of a landlord in Uttar Pradesh, his belly rolling over his pajama chord as he ordered serfs to set his surplus grain on fire. Feeling had come upon him that he was creating the world, that the bodies he occupied acted at his command; the thoughts he jumped inside were his. He invented a world where he could take the central position. But Saleem the narrator developed a hindsight 'born of the instinct of self-preservation' (175). He should project his identity from the 'massed identities' of the multitudes which threatened to engulf him and annihilate his existence.

Ahmed Sinai remained as cold as ice since the freezing of his assets. He lost interest in his wife and found himself involved in the fantasy of the tetrapods. He invested money and avoided publicity. But Narlikar's sudden death in mob violence led to Ahmed Sinai's financial ruin. His health declined and within a few months he turned white. He was secretly pleased by his transformation into a white man. It was the 'pigmentation disorder' which affected a large number of Indian businessmen in the early years of independence. All over India, fortunes of good Indian businessman were thriving thanks to the accumulation of black money in the wake of the First Five-Year Plan. The businessmen of India turning white which may be termed as 'pigmentation disorder' suggests metaphorically the process of westernization and serves as a moral allegory for the post-colonial history of the nation. Link between his personal history and the history of the nation looks co-incidental. Rushdie's deconstruction of the official account of the history takes the form of parodic representation. Historical facts like India's launching of Five-Year Plans or linguistic division of the country have been fictionalized and mixed with fantasy. Pigmentation disorder in respect of his father Ahmed Sinai and other businessmen of the newly independent country has been comically and satirically described. By drawing parallels between the happenings in his life and the life of his family members and the happenings outside in the life of the new nation, private and public experiences are politicized.

LOVE IN BOMBAY

Saleem's psychic travels in the broken-down tower being over, the narrative gives a fascinating account of Saleem's falling in love with a white girl. She is Evie Burns, an American girl. She came to Bombay on the New Year's Day of 1957 to stay with her father. She lived in an apartment block built for the foreigners on the lower reaches of the Methwold Estate. She was a knife-sharp girl with grotesque figure—'her hair was made of scarecrow straw, her skin was peppered with freckles and her teeth lived in a metal cage' (181). Saleem's infatuation with Evie was brief and it coincided with the historical event of the linguistic division of Bombay. Besides, Saleem's disastrous love affair with an American girl serves as a parody for India's short-lived romance with America during the 1950s when India received large quantities of American aid. When she first appeared at Methwold Estate, Evie gave the airs of her superiority to the Indian neighbours. She was armed with a pistol and arrived at the circus ring on a bicycle to make a display of her cycling skill. She established her supremacy over the Indians who stood amazed and accepted their new boss. Our hero, Saleem fell in love with this unmanageable girl in the fashion of Bombay film. It was love at first sight and he remained tongue-tied in her presence. He did not have enough courage to express his emotion and, in a grotesque mimicry of European fashion approached his bosom friend Sonny Ibrahim to plead his case to her. Sonny agreed to plead Saleem's case. Sonny gathered some experience in the art of love making though it was not a happy one. He fell in love with Saleem's tempestuous sister Brass Monkey who was so enraged by his protestation of love that she publicly disgraced him with the help of her European friends. However, Sonny agreed to plead love on behalf of Saleem. Enough materials for farce. But then pleading or canvassing one's private feeling coincides with the act of public canvassing in an election campaign. It was 1957 and the campaigns for general election had begun. The political parties of India like Jan Sangh, Congress, Communists and regional parties like DMK started their election campaign. This campaign rhetoric farcically describes Saleem's indirect courtship for Evie. Sonny started canvassing his friend's 'chosen constituency and heard the voice of the electorate' (221). Erie Burns scornfully rejected Saleem's offer of love. 'That sniffer! He can't even ride a bike' (222). The defeated candidate for Evie's love did not lose heart at the rejection of his first love but decided to share her interest in cycle riding. The temptation of Evie Burns drew him to the circus ring. Evie was teaching the Methwold children her bicycle arts. During one such trial run, Evie gave Saleem such a push that his cycle was out of his control and ran across the ring to clash with Sonny Ibrahim. Saleem fell on the ground and got an injury in the head. The circus ring accident did complete what the washing-chest accident had begun. It unlocked the door of his head to the other midnight's children, 'they were in my head, in the front row—sending their here-I-am signals, from north south east west—the other children born during that midnight hour' (223). During his convalescence from the severe injury he received in the bicycle accident Saleem's parents took him to Agra for a family reunion. There he learnt from the rickshaw puller Rashid, the techniques of cycle riding and found on the top of his grandfather's almirah, the moth-eaten perforated sheet.

And now the narrative gives a journalistic account of an historical event, the language riots of 1957. In 1955, the states reorganization committee submitted its report to Mr Nehru and a year later, its recommendation had been implemented. 'India had been divided anew, into fourteen states and six centrally administered territories. But the boundaries of these states were not formed by rivers, or mountains or any natural features of the terrain; they were instead walls of words' (189). The committee did not consider the state of Bombay province and this led to violent protest and mass demonstration. The United Maharashtra Party stood for the Marathi language and demanded the state of Maharashtra while Great Gujarat Party stood for Gujarati language and demanded the creation of a state to the north of the city of Bombay. Methwold Estate was cut off from the rest of the city of Bombay by a two-day long protest march of the supporters of Marathi language. From the hilltop, the children of the Estate under the leadership of Evie Burns took a look at the procession of the language marchers. Saleem seized the opportunity and tried to impress Evie by the demonstration of his newly acquired cycling skill. An irate Evie gave him a hard push and Saleem hurtled down the slope and made his first foray into history crashing into the procession of the language marchers on a runaway bicycle. It was a Marathi speaking mob and some rowdy youths asked Saleem to speak some Gujarati words 'the little laad-Sahib...from the big, rich hill' (191), they mocked. But Saleem's Gujarati was as bad as Marathi. To save himself from embarrassment, he repeated a rhyme designed to make fun of the speech rhythm of the language.

Soo che? Saru che!
Danda le ke maru che!

[How are you?—I am well—I'll take a stick and thrash you to hell!]. It was a nonsensical rhyme but the Marathi language marchers took it as a war cry against the Gujarati demonstrators. 'The two parties fell upon one another with no little zeal, and to the tune of my little rhyme the first of the language riots got under way, fifteen killed and over three hundred wounded' (192). Thus Saleem became indirectly responsible for triggering of the violence which ended with the partition of the state of Bombay. But ironically Saleem became cured of the Evie Burns disease. The love bug left him. It is the women, who make and unmake him.

MY TENTH BIRTHDAY

On his tenth birthday in 1957 Saleem became aware of the fact that five hundred and eighty-one other children of the midnight were celebrating their birthdays, too; which was how he understood the secret of his original hour of birth. Saleem's tenth birth was a low-key affair, attended by his family and a few classmates. Hilltop boys at the instance of an embittered Evie Burns boycotted it. Saleem was undaunted by this boycott of the hilltop gang and he formed his own gang of midnight's children who were spread over the length and breadth of the country. His brain became the headquarters of Midnight Children's Conference, M.C.C. Metaphorically, Saleem's tenth birthday coincides with the tenth independence day of the newly born state. The tenth birthday of the new nation witnessed disasters like storms, floods and hailstones from a cloudless sky which wrecked the rhetoric of Second Five-Year Plan.

Padma, who had gone out of the narrative out of her feeling of disappointment at Saleem's sickness returned with 'herbs of virility' (193) which she had collected from a holy man during her absence. Driven to craziness because of her unconsummated love, she made an attempt to awaken Saleem's manhood. The herbs failed to resuscitate his masculine power and he was driven to delirious fever for a week. Saleem did not blame Padma nor did he doubt her love. Now Padma is back and his narrative gains balance and proportion. Padma's excursion into the world of ancient wisdom (magic and fantasy) in search of love—potions works as a bridge between the narrator Saleem and the 'world of ancient learning' (194). Padma's pre-occupation with earthiness, love and marriage forces Saleem back into the world of linear narrative. 'This love, mister, will drive a woman to craziness'—Padma wails (194). Padma is referred to as 'the Lotus Goddess' and a co-creator of the fictional universe. After her return, Saleem's narrative gets its balance as it embraces Indian concept of time and the myth of cosmic creation and multiple fantasies. The narrative thus presents a collage of the western genre and the mythic/folkloric Indian tradition. It becomes a realistic hybrid and secular post-modern tale which may euphemistically be called magic realism. The narrator protagonist Saleem reaches the 'fantastic heart' (195) of his story which gives the novel its title—the midnight's children. 'I am at my table once again, once again Padma sits at my feet, urging me on. I am balanced once more' (195). It's an Indian tale and Rushdie's magic realism is based on Indian view of reality which is pluralistic and mythical. It incorporates Hindu, Islamic and Christian motifs and symbols, and artistically undermines the purist representation of Man and World.

During the first hour of August 15, 1947 between midnight and 1.00 A.M.—no less than one thousand and one children were born within the frontiers of the newly born country. The number 1001 is symbolic but what matters is not the symbol but the nature of the children born. Each one of the children was endowed with special features and miraculous faculties. A number of these children failed to survive. Malnutrition, disease and misfortune accounted for the death of four hundred and twenty children. Number 420 has been, since time immemorial associated with fraud, deception and trickery. By 1957 the surviving five hundred and eighty one children were nearing their tenth birthday wholly ignorant of one another's existence when Saleem became aware of them as a consequence of the bicycle accident. Another noteworthy feature of the children was that the closer to midnight their birth-times were, the greater were their powers. The children born in the last moment of the midnight hour were no more than 'circus freak, twins and bearded girls' (198). Those born towards the half hour of the midnight were gifted with useful faculties like the powers of healing. The children, who arrived in the first minute after midnight, were given 'the highest talents of which men had ever dreamed' (199) like gifts of prophecy, time-travelling and sorcery. Two of them, Saleem and Shiva who were born on the stroke of midnight hour were endowed with the greatest talents of all. 'Shiva and Saleem, nose and knees and knees and nose... to Shiva, the hour had given the gifts of war and to me, the greatest talent of all—the ability to look into the hearts and minds of men' (200). The midnight children with their miraculous talents turned out to be a metaphor for 'a thousand and one possibilities' (200) offered by history at the moment of independence, and also, one thousand and one ways of looking at things. 'Midnight's children can be made to represent many things...they can be seen as the last throw of everything antiquated and retrogressive in our myth-ridden nation...or as the true hope of freedom' (200).

Padma's amazement is understandable. The fantasy underlying the birth of midnight's children strains her credulity. 'O, baba! You are sick; what have you said?,' was her incredulous response to the tale. So Saleem is engaged in an effort to defend his fantastical and metaphorical narrative. Saleem pleads to her non-believing audience. 'Reality can have metaphorical content; that does not make it less real' (200). The reader should not make the mistake of dismissing his narrative as mere delirium or the product of a sick mind. What he narrated is literal truth and not the 'bazarre creation of a rumbling, diseased mind' (200). Fathered by history, midnight's children represented the promise of a new feature 'as though...history arriving at a point of the highest significance and promise, had chosen to sow, in that instant, the seeds of a future which would genuinely differ from anything the world had seen up to that time' (195).

AT THE PIONEER CAFÉ

Saleem's story veers round to the dream world of politics and film. The Pioneer Café in Bombay became a repository of many dreams. It was a favourite haunt of the film stars, goondas, taxi drivers and smugglers. The Pioneer was the focus of the city's ambitious persons, dreamers and a 'notorious Communist Party hangout' (216). Amina's ex-husband Nadir Khan, a rhymeless poet transformed himself into a communist leader. He acquired a new name Qasim Khan like his former wife Mumtaz who was known as Amina after she became the wife of Ahmed Sinai. Now Qasim Khan was an official candidate of the Communist Party in the general election held in 1957 and he used to visit the Pioneer Café in the afternoon. On her part, Amina got tired and bored as her husband and Ahmed Sinai failed to recover from the effects of the freezing of his assets, and became cold and unemotional in his relation with his wife. After his tenth birthday, Saleem observed that his mother Amina, on receiving a wrong number telephone call, disappeared on shopping trips. He followed her, hidden like a 'stowaway' (214) in the boot of the family car and arrived at the Pioneer Café which was situated near the film studios in north Bombay. Saleem watched through the 'glassy cinema screen' (216) of the Pioneer Café's window. His suspicion of his mother's perfidy was confirmed as he saw his mother Amina and her ex-husband playing out their love-scenes. Saleem lodged himself in his mother's thoughts; he rode in his mother's head and thus sat in the Pioneer Café and heard conversations about the electoral prospects of Quasim, the red. Thus disembodied, he trailed his mother as she accompanied Quasim on his electioneering tours and moved amongst the destitute on behalf of the Communist Party. Saleem imagined himself in the role of the legendary Caliph, Haroun al-Rashid who did enjoy moving incognito amongst the people of Baghdad. He lodged himself in Amina's thoughts and followed her through her ways. Saleem was shocked at her mother's infidelity but perhaps she did it because of growing impoverishment of her own life.

'Frailty, thy name is woman', Saleem experiences Hamletian disgust and confusion of mind and spirit. This is more so as his imagined ladylove Evie Burns banished him from his private hideout. He, as an alternative, began to commune with midnight's children telepathically at night. During one such meeting of the children of the midnight held in the parliament of his brain, Saleem encountered Shiva, the genetic son of Amina and Ahmed Sinai who had now been brought up in poverty and was filled with violent resentment and anger against the scheme of things in this unjust world. His putative father Wee Willie Winkie died and he had to struggle hard since his childhood, for survival. Shiva became the leader of a notorious gang in Bombay's underworld. Shiva met Saleem in the Midnight's Children's Conference (MCC) and was filled with rage and claimed joint leadership by virtue of the fact that he also was born at exactly the midnight hour. But Saleem turned down Shiva's proposal as according to him MCC was 'a loose federation of equals' (220). Saleem continued to win Shiva to his point of view. 'The thing is, we must be here for a purpose...there has to be a reason' (220). Shiva ridiculed Saleem's ideas of reason and purpose and mocked at the rich boy, Saleem whose head was, as he thought, full of crazy staff. Shiva questions Saleem's narrative, rather meta-narrative of reason and purpose. 'What purpose, man? What thing in the whole world got reason? For what reason you're rich and I'm poor? Where's the reason in starving, man?' (220). The rivalry between Saleem and Shiva, nose and knees, the rich and the poor, the mainstream and the regions, the centre and the periphery, that began that night would have far-reaching consequences in the life of the nation in the succeeding years. The chaos in the parliament of MCC held in Saleem's brain metaphorically reflects the state of Indian parliament in post-colonial times. Shiva embodies the force of violence and anarchy, and thus poses a threat to the concept of secular and liberal democracy as represented by Saleem. Together they embody the contradictory forces which propel Indian democracy and politics even today. Shiva and his gang helped the ruling party to rig the election of 1957 in Bombay. The hoodlums and gangsters threatened the voters to keep them away from the polling stations on election day. Qasim Khan was defeated but the Communists emerged as the largest single opposition party in the parliament.

But then the narrator Saleem is not under obligation to give a factual account of history and politics. He discovers another factual error in his story. 1957 general election was held before his tenth birthday and not after. His memory plays tricks on him but he stubbornly refuses to 'alter the sequence of events' (222). He clings to the subjective vision of reality. He values the memory's version of events more than the literal facts of history. He tries to convince Padma of his narratorial right to be unreliable. 'Padma, if you are a little uncertain of my reliability, well, a little uncertainty is no bad thing' (212). There are many versions of reality and truth, and, it is undesirable to impose one's views of things on others. Memory becomes the only representative of truth. It is memory's truth which 'selects, eliminates, alters, exaggerates, minimizes...but in the end...creates its own reality, its heterogeneous but usually coherent vision of events' (211). Saleem, the narrator, foregrounds memory which serves as a tool for reclamation of the past and re-creation of history.

ALPHA AND OMEGA

Saleem practises detachment from the happenings around him. There are events and more events which demand inclusion in his narrative. It becomes increasingly difficult for him to keep pace with the happenings all around. 'There are beginnings here and all manner of ends' (223). There is the end of Evie Burns' dominion over the children of Methwold Estate. After the general election of 1957 there was widespread political turmoil in Bombay. Government's failure to implement the linguistic division of Bombay led to riots between the Marathi and Gujarati speakers of the languages. There was a series of explosions in the city's central reservoir which resulted in the acute scarcity of water and a 'great cat invasion' (224). The stray cats began to assemble in the relatively better-off areas of the city. An army of thirsty cats invaded Methwold Estate while the people living there thought that it was 'the end of the world' (224). There was violence and turmoil in the air and Saleem immersed himself in the thoughts inside his head. "I shall take wings (like the parahamsa gander who can soar out of the element into another) and return, briefly, to the affairs of my inner world" (227). Like the mythical gander the 'parahamsa', Saleem found that he did inhabit two worlds 'Awake I was obliged to face the multiple miseries of maternal perfidy and paternal decline, of the fickleness of friendship and the varied tyrannies of school, asleep, I was at the centre of the most exciting world any child had ever discovered' (227). Saleem occasionally fell into a trance, 'Samadhi' and envisaged the ills of life, the flesh is heir to.

With the increase of his telepathic power, Saleem found that he could pick up the midnight's children's transmissions and broadcast his own messages and also he could 'act as a sort of national network' (227). He easily turned his brain into a forum where all the children could talk to one another, through his mind. In the early days of 1958, five hundred and eighty-one children of the midnight did assemble, for one hour, between midnight and 1 a.m. in the parliament of his brain. It was a motley group, an undisciplined bunch of five hundred and eighty-one ten-year-olds who assembled in the Lok Sabha of Saleem's brain and selected him as their leader. There was rivalry between Saleem and Shiva over the question of leadership in the parliament of children. But the issue was eventually decided in Saleem's favour because he possessed the quality of leadership. He told the conference that they should be guided by 'reason' and 'purpose' in their discussion of the issues of general importance. 'We must think what we are for.' Child narrator's speech in the conference, who happens to be the leader of the house, is a parody of the midnight oration of the first Prime Minister of the newly independent nation, in the assembly hall at the midnight hour of August 15. The child members who assembled in the conference held into the brain of their leader, hotly debated issues ranging from collectivism and individualism to science and religion. The debates metaphorically reflected the disagreement and division of opinions among the members of the parliament of the newly independent nation on issues of general well-being. But then as Saleem observes, the children, despite their miraculous gifts, remained to his mind, 'a sort of many headed monster, speaking in the myriad tongues of Babel; they were the very essence of multiplicity' (229). They evinced unlike their seniors, natural exuberance and youthful optimism. None of them could think that 'the purpose of midnight's children might be annihilation; that they would have no meaning until they were destroyed' (229).

The children born at the midnight hour or for that matter, Saleem, the principal protagonist felt the 'painful, engrossing torture of growing up' (229) in the newly independent nation. He suffered mutilation of his body at school at the hands of his geography teacher Emil Zagallo. In a geography class Saleem incurred his anger as he protested against the teacher's harassment of a brilliant classmate. An infuriated teacher dragged Saleem by his hair to the front of the class. It was an act of cruel irony on the part of the teacher when he started teaching the students human geography by displaying Saleem's hideous face to the students. 'In the face of the ugly ape don't you see the whole map of India? (231). The mischievous teacher explained to the class that Saleem's chin stood for the southern peninsula and the disfiguring birthmarks on his face represented the two wings of Pakistan. The crudity of the teacher's joke equated Saleem's misshapen body with the national map of India. The violence of the geography teacher was responsible for the loss of his hair. The furious teacher seized a tuft of his hair and pulled it out creating a blood-filled patch on Saleem's head. Zagallo lost his job but left a legacy of Saleem's 'monkish tonsure,' 'baldie' and 'map face' (232). The first mutilation was followed by the second. In a skirmish with his classmates, Saleem lost the middle finger of his right hand and was admitted to a hospital. The doctors advised an emergency transfusion of blood in his body. On examination of his blood it was revealed that it was neither Alpha nor Omega, neither A (his mother's blood group) nor O (his father's) and it was unlike the blood of his parents, it was rhesus—negative. This startling disclosure had an overwhelming effect on his life. 'Suddenly you are forever other than you were; and the world becomes such that parents can cease to be parents, and love can turn to hate' (237). The ten-year-old child narrator sitting on the hospital bed with a bandaged finger was seen brooding over the mystery of blood, certainties, identities and meaning of existence. But then Saleem's mother shrieked, 'But of course you must believe me, doctor, my God, of course he is our son!' (237)

The narrator Saleem is endowed with the benefits of hindsight. His narrative becomes unconventional as it destroys the unities and conventions of fine writing. It dawns upon him that a human being inside himself is anything but a whole that he is anything but homogeneous and, he is one person one minute and another the next. Human body also is not homogeneous as the fact of the loss of his finger and removal of his hair from his head amply illustrate. This fragmentation of one's private self has consequences on public sphere of action as well.

THE KOLYNOS KID

Saleem finds that he has been the sort of a person to whom things have been done. The discovery that he was not the true son of his parents left him shattered. The narrator hero, rather anti-hero, it appears, is of illegitimate birth. Saleem Sinai, the perennial victim of history persists in seeing himself as the protagonist. But like the other children of midnight, Saleem, the most gifted child has no place in the active mode, because he is a victim of events and 'handcuffed to history.' Consequent upon the loss of his finger and the discovery of his blood, Saleem is temporarily abandoned by his parents. Uncle Hanif and his ayah Mary appeared in the hospital to collect him. Saleem finds that something has gone wrong with his world. Now he is in exile in the small apartment of Uncle Hanif and aunt Pia, near Marine Drive. He has no part in his birth; he is a victim of the situation and accepts the banishment uncomplainingly. Saleem looks upon himself as the Kolynos Kid, a gleam toothed boy on a hoarding near Kemp's Corner announcing the merits of Kolynos tooth paste by squeezing an 'inexhaustible tube' (240). Saleem's role is identical with the role of 'an involuntary Kolynos Kid' who had been 'squeezing crises and transformations out of a bottomless tube...on to his metaphorical tooth brush' (240). Hanif and Pia had no child born to them and hence they accepted the abandoned child with affection and love in their heart. Saleem has always been a victim to whom things are done but he makes a playful explanation of his claim to a 'place at the center of things' (238). His central position has been ratified by the prime minister. Nehru in his letter congratulated the baby Saleem and identified him with the newly born state. 'Your life, which will be in a sense, the mirror of our own' (238). Thirty years later, Saleem starts experiencing the mutilation and fragmentation of his body and tries to understand in his own way how the life of a single individual can influence and reflect the life of a nation. The narrative provides a pseudo-scientific answer to the question of the identification of the individual and the newly independent state. 'I was linked to history both literally and metaphorically, both actively and passively, in what our scientists might turn 'modes of connection' composed of 'dualistically-combined configurations' of the two pairs of opposite adverbs' (238). To explain the connection, hyphens are necessary: actively-literally, passively-metaphorically, actively-metaphorically and passively-literally. Midnight's children were inextricably entwined with their world.

Saleem was related to the nation 'actively-literally' when his action like intervention in the language riot directly influenced the course of history. His link with the country 'passively-metaphorically' may be established in the connection between the child Saleem's programme of self-enlargement and the infant nation's heroic programme for growth. His relation with the state 'passively-literally' suggests the historical events that affected him and his family like the freezing of the property of Ahmed Sinai by the state and followed by the freezing of his emotion. 'Actively-metaphorically' Saleem's fate was entwined with the fate of the secular democratic country. The mutilation of his finger and cracks and fissures in his body corresponded to the cracking up of the state. It is only in 'passive-metaphorical' mode of connection that Saleem assumes his central position as a witness and chronicler.

In his new role, Saleem acted out the 'part of the surrogate son' (243) to his uncle and aunt Pia. His stay in his uncle's house was for him 'to exist in the hot sticky heart of a Bombay talkie' (243). By that time Hanif's and Pia's career in the cinema was on the decline. Hanif began to despise the 'myth-life' of India which provided life and sustenance to Bombay film. He started writing a realistic film about a pickle factory run by women. He was conscious of the pernicious effects of myth and fantasy in the Bombay film on the life and mind of the people of a newly independent state which made a pledge of secularism and modernism. Independence at the midnight hour gave the nation an opportunity to come out of the shadow of the 'fabulous antiquity' of Hindu India and become a modern and secular state by espousing multiplicity and plurality. Dream of the founding fathers in the succeeding years started to fade. Many-headed monster raised its ugly head. Regional, religious, linguistic and caste-based loyalties were uppermost in the minds of the people of the republic, and the country's secular and democratic body politic developed cracks and fissures.

The narrator is prophetic. It is the author Rushdie who speaks—

> In that time of accelerated events and diseased hours, the past of India rose up to confound her present; the

> new born secular state was being given an awesome reminder of its fabulous antiquity...so that people were seized by atavistic longings, and forgetting the new myth of freedom reverted to their old ways, their old regionalist loyalties and prejudices, and the body politic began to crack (245).

Rise of coalition governance in politics, fundamentalism in the field of religion and regional intolerance in the last part of the twentieth century and after, confirm the authorial apprehension about the fate of the nation.

COMMANDER SABARMATI'S BATON

Saleem's exile in his uncle's apartment was over and he returned home accompanied by his mother Amina. His loathing for his adulterous mother was joined with his extreme dislike of Homi Catrack who seduced and then abandoned his beautiful aunt, Pia. He was possessed of a revenge motive which would have grave consequence on his family and the nation. On his return, Saleem found himself in 'an atmosphere of confusion and distrust' (253). His importance in the family had been usurped by his sister Brass Monkey. His parents' loss of interest in him gave him greater freedom. He felt the transformations that were taking place in every aspect of his life, symptoms of adolescence appearing on his body. He had attained adult height. Saleem was coming out of infancy; he was growing to be an adult. Midnight's children were becoming grown ups. The miraculous children of the midnight cannot be thought of as immune to the vices of their parents and 'the prejudices and world-views of adults began to take over their minds' (254). As a result, the Midnight Children's Conference started disintegrating. The initial excitement and enthusiasm were becoming replaced by boredom and dissension which only widened the cracks and fissures in the conference. The poison of the elders leaked into the children's conference and pulled the children apart. 'I found children from Maharashtra loathing Gujaratis and fair-skinned northerners reviling Dravidian 'blackies'; there were religious rivalries; and class entered our councils' (254). In this way the Midnight Children's Conference ironically fulfilled the prophecy of the Prime Minister Nehru and became in truth, 'a mirror of the nation.' The Children's Conference fell prey to the paradoxes of the third world nationalism, it's 'endless duality of masses and classes, capital and labour, them and us' (255). Saleem cried passionately and made desperate pleas to overcome the differences and forge a third principle. Only by being other, by being new, can the children fulfil the promise of their birth. The magical gifts seemed powerless to prevent the force of conflict and dissension which tore the council apart. There was no taker for Saleem's third principle. The duality persisted. The rivalry between the idealistic Saleem and practical Shiva eventually led to the disintegration of Midnight's Children's Conference. Shiva seized the moment of victory. For Shiva, the world was not ideas but things. 'There is no third principle, there is only money and poverty, have and lack, right and left, me against the world' (255). Thus the children's parliament got poisoned by the discord and cynism of the adult world and its institutions like Lok Sabha. Childhood was killed and the miraculous talents and gifts at birth notwithstanding, Saleem found it impossible to mould and shape things differently. His growing body showed a propensity to fall into fragments. 'If there is a third principle, its name is childhood. But it dies; or rather, it is murdered' (255). Thought of revenge or murder haunted Saleem, no doubt. A two-headed monster was lurking inside him. He was to teach his hypocritical mother a lesson and avenge the treachery of his promiscuous neighbour, Homi Catrack. Lust for revenge draws a human closer to a snake. Snake imagery is very powerful to explain revenge motive. Saleem learnt from the European snake expert about 'occult powers of snakes' (257) and their ways of attacking the enemy. 'Imitate the action of the snake...strike from the cover of a bush' (258). By using his gift of telepathic power, Saleem began to spy on his enemy, Homi Catrack and his fancy woman, Lila Sabarmati, the beautiful wife of the 'heir apparent to the title of Admiral of the Fleet' (258). He collected the details of their weekly rendezvous in an apartment near Colaba Causeway, and after cutting pieces out of newspaper reporting, framed and sent an anonymous note to Commander Sabarmati. 'Cutting up history to suit (his) nefarious purposes' (259). History does not only present objective truth but can be manipulated to constitute a subjective view of reality and serve individual purposes. What moved him into action were maternal hypocrisy and the grief of his aunt. He wanted to teach 'a lesson to all unfaithful wives and mothers' (262). But then Saleem's 'first attempt at rearranging history' (260) caused the greatest public scandal of his time.

Proceeding on the clue, Commander Sabarmati reached the apartment block with a gun in hand. Lita answered the door, he shot her twice in the stomach. She fell backwards, he marched past her and found her lover Homi Catrack and shot him in the genitals, in the heart and through the right eye. Homi died on the spot. The revenge drama was over. The gun-waving naval officer surrendered himself to a traffic Sergeant. The policeman fled in panic and there was traffic confusion. Sabarmati with the gun in hand rose to the podium and 'He began to direct Cars, using the smoking gun as a baton' (262). This was how he was found at the time of his arrest. This incident moved the people's imagination. There was tremendous hue and cry in the country. During Sabarmati's trial, public opinion worked in favour of the cuckolded husband. 'Commander Sabarmati was the most popular murderer in the history of Indian jurisprudence. Husbands acclaimed his punishment of an errant wife; faithful women felt justified in their fidelity' (262). The murder of the wife's seducer was, in the public eyes, compared to Ram's slaughter of Sita's abductor, Ravana. 'If Rama himself were alive, would we send him to prison for slaying the abductor of Sita?' (264). Thus Saleem's 'vengeful irruption into history' gave rise to a national crisis. The country was faced with a choice between the rule of heroism and the rule of law, between the mythical past and its democratic present. In the end the rule of law prevailed and Sabarmati was sent to prison. The Sabarmati judgment becomes a salutary reminder of the fact that we live in a modern society which is governed by the rule of law. We have traveled a long way from our mythical past. Norms of life followed in the epic ages should not constitute the ways of life at the current time. That we have outgrown our mythic self explains our rationality, civilization and our belief in the rule of law. Saleem's revenge motive did have the desired effect on his mother. She stopped answering wrong number telephone calls. One other consequence of the Sabarmati episode was that all the inmates of Methwold Estate sold their houses to the Narlikar women and left. Ahmed Sinai was left alone with his family. In August 1958 Saleem realized that the world of his childhood had come to an end.

REVELATIONS

Saleem's narrative gains momentum. He understands that he must finish his tale before he faces decay. The narrator strives to achieve reliability through the tender ministration of his dear mistress narratee Padma. Saleem now enters a difficult period of his life when 'revelations flowed faster than blood' (271).

During the Sabarmati trial and the resultant hue and cry the scandal generated, Dr Dubash, the nuclear physicist met with his accidental death. His son Cyrus Dubash was Saleem's bosom friend and he was the most brilliant one. But at the instance of his fanatic mother, Cyrus Dubash transformed himself into the richest child Guru in India. He was metamorphosed from a 'school prodigy' into the 'most successful holy child in history' (269). He became Cyrus-the-great who had a nuclear physicist for a father and a religious fanatic for a mother. He lectured American disciples, amassed large fortune and finally was drowned at sea while attempting to walk over water. This serves as a parody of the role of Mahaguru in Indian life. The revelation of the child-Guru Cyrus was followed by a series of revelations. Towards the end of 1957, the Narlikar women group started demolishing the colonial palaces of the Methwold Estate. They forced Ahmed Sinai to sell his house. Buckingham Villa the Sinai household was enveloped in the dust. When danger comes, it comes in battalions. At such a time, the Sinais received shocking news from Pia. Hanif Aziz had committed suicide. Deprived of the income he received from Homi Catrack, who was killed, Haniff jumped off the roof of the Marine Drive apartment block. The family members gathered at the Buckingham Villa amidst dust storm to observe the forty-day mourning. Pia sat like stone though everyone including Emerald and Zulfikar who had come from Pakistan cried profusely. Only Hanif's wife Pia behaved unusually. There was an expectation that an actress of her standing would respond to her widowhood in high style. But contrary to all expectations, Pia remained dry-eyed and composed. Hanif hated melodrama and so did Pia, his widowed wife. Hanif the serious filmmaker lodged a protest against the melodramatic and unreal world of Bombay film through his suicide. Hanif's death was a terrible shock for his old parents. Reverend mother announced her decision to migrate to Pakistan with her husband Aadam Aziz and his daughter-in-law Pia. But Dr Aziz, an old man of sixty-eight years declined to go to Pakistan because that was a country built especially for God. Aadam Aziz was now after revenge against God who took away his son. His God died young and left a hole in his heart. Over the years, Dr Aziz had declined. Two days later the old man made a contrary revelation that he had 'seen with his own eyes the God in whose death he had tried all his life to believe' (275). He saw in his dream the boatman Tai and Hummingbird who was killed by the fanatics. Aziz's loss of optimism after the death of Hummingbird, his disappointment with the new nation and his growing submission to his wife's fanaticism had taken a heavy toll on his body and mind. Gradually his bones started disintegrating and his body developed cracks and fissures like the new nation. Grandfather's disease of disintegration of body would eventually leak into Saleem. Dr Aziz was visited by apparition who had asked him 'you're the one whose son died' (276). The old man never forgave God who had snatched his son from him. He was filled with the revenge motive. The narrative gives a lucid description of Aadam Aziz's revenge and death in Kashmir which coincided with the theft of the holy relic from the Hazratbal mosque of Srinagar in 1963. The communal disturbances which occurred in the subcontinent following the theft might be read as an 'attempt at revenge upon God by a father who had lost his son' (277). On January 1, 1964, Dr Aziz climbed the hill on which

Sankara temple stood with a stick in hand. But he could not enter the inner sanctum of the temple to take revenge upon God. His bones disintegrated and he died. Then Aziz's story of reckoning with God ended where it began in his youth when he left the valley with a hole in the heart created by his loss of faith. The death of the patriarch coincided with a national tragedy. Prime Minister Nehru fell ill and he did not recover. The fatal sickness claimed his life on May 27, 1964.

Mary made a revelation in 1958 which changed the course of Saleem's life. Mary saw in her dream the ghost of Joseph and was unnerved. She ran to Amina, threw herself at her feet and cried for mercy. Before the members of the Sinai family Mary made a confession of her long suppressed crime. Saleem was not the genetic son of Amina and Ahmed Sinai. His real parents were Wee Willie Winkie and Vanita. Mary's confession made all the members stupefied and amazed. This revelation dragged the family members out of the charmed world invented by Mary with the change of name-tags eleven years ago. Mary left Buckingham Villa for good. Her confession made Saleem enter into another exile in Pakistan.

MOVEMENTS PERFORMED BY PEPPERPOTS

Mary Pereira's revelation was for Saleem the end of his innocence and beginning of experience. The information that he was not the genetic son of Amina and Ahmed Sinai but a usurper of the position of Shiva for eleven long years turned his world upside down. He became afraid; he would not be able to conceal from Shiva the secrets of his birth. He resolved that his destructive alter ego should never again enter the Council of the Midnight Children's Conference. He banished Shiva from the parliament of his mind, the conference hall of the Midnight's Children. After banishing Shiva from the council of the children, Saleem found himself thrown across the border and lost his connection with the Midnight's Children. Saleem's exile in Pakistan was hastened by the commotion in the Sinai family following Mary's startling disclosure.

Late in September 1958, the mourning period of Hanif Aziz came to an end. Ahmed Sinai emerged from his 'private world of abstraction' (283) and directed his violent rage at his wife. He ranted at Amina for hours within the hearing of the family because he held Amina responsible for Mary's confession. Reverend mother came to defend her daughter, clutching Saleem to her bosom, she legitimized him and advised his daughter Amina to leave an inadequate husband. She instructed her second daughter Emerald to take Amina and her children, Saleem and Brass Monkey and even Hanif's widowed wife Pia to Pakistan soon along with her husband Emerald looked displeased but she did not have courage to oppose her mother. Saleem left his life-long home along with his mother who was not his mother, a sister and aunt Pia leaving Ahmed Sinai to his lonely fate. He left his home with the knowledge of his birth and entered the country of his exile and received the 'grudging hospitality' of his aunt Emerald and her husband Zulfikar. The experience of the journey from Bombay to Rawalpindi was to Saleem a travel from warmth of life to coldness of heart. Besides, General Zulfikar's lavishly decorated military bungalow was devoid of the feel of life. In this dull and lifeless house, the Sinais and Pia felt small, useless and 'non-productive members' (286). The most important inhabitant of this lifeless house was a dog. This dog named Bonzo demonstrated her gifts of smelling out mines in a minefield on the Indo-Pakistani border and was drafted into the army as a 'four legged mine-detector with the courtesy rank of sergeant major' (286). Zulfikar's prowess is parodied when he is shown to be the father of a son named Zafar who wetted his pants throughout his adult life and brought shame on his family.

Saleem's schooling in Pakistan began. He went to school with Zafar. On the other hand, Amina started withering in her exile while making a hard struggle to re-imagine and re-build her relationship with Saleem who was her son and not her son. Brass Monkey, on her part, tried to re-imagine her brother. But it was an exercise fraught with tension. Saleem could detect a distance in her mother's and sister's gentleness to him. The feeling of guilt and remorse in the personal level of existence was, to some extent, mitigated by Saleem's involvement in public events. An eleven-year-old boy witnessed Pakistan's transformation from a parliamentary democracy into a military dictatorship through a midnight coup which was planned in a dinner party at his uncle General Zulfikar's house. But then parliamentary democracy and the Godly country of Pakistan go ill together. Democracy in the subcontinent till the day, remains a farce with the erosion of values in public life, opportunism and rampant corruption. Saleem attended the dinner party as a relative of Zulfikar and helped 'active metaphorically' (291) to change the fate of Pakistan. On the night of October 7, 1958 General Ayub Khan appeared in the dinner party and declared the end of the civilian rule and imposition of the martial law in Pakistan. Army officers present in the dinner party only gave a nod. Saleem's uncle Zulfikar demonstrated before the officers, the movement of the army with the pepperpots on the dining table and Saleem assisted him in this business of moving pepperpots. 'General Zulfikar described troop movement; I moved pepperpots symbolically while he spoke' (290). Ayub Khan assumed control of the state. The narrative constitutes a parody of a revolution which overthrew an elected Government in Pakistan. Uncle Zulfikar was pleased with Saleem and treated him as his own son. Thus Saleem created a new father for himself. 'Zulfikar became the latest in the line of men who have been willing to call me...my son' (290). The narrative presents a critique of the topsy-turvy political situation in Pakistan *vis-à-vis* the midnight coup which is described as the 'revolution of the pepperpots' (285). Intrigue and treason are the hallmark of Pakistani politics. 'Midnight has many children; the offspring of independence were not all human. Violence, corruption, poverty, generals, chaos, greed and pepperpots...I had to go into exile to learn that the children of midnight were more varied than I...had dreamed' (291). During the four years of exile, his sister Brass Monkey was transformed into a submissive girl and a good singer. Saleem observed the transformation of his sister from a wild and unruly girl into a docile and submissive adolescent. At her fourteenth birthday party, she sang in a matured and nice voice and earned a name 'Jamila Singer'. It was during her exile in Pakistan, Brass Monkey made a break with the secular legacy of her grandfather and fell in love with God and fanaticism.

DRAINAGE AND THE DESERT

Amina left her husband Ahmed Sinai to his lonely fate and departed for the Godly Country of Pakistan. Children also left their father. As a result, Ahmed Sinai—steadily fell into decline and a state of drunkenness. There was no human companion except his secretary Alice Pereira. Four years of stay in the Methwold Estate saw Ahmed Sinai besieged by loneliness, fear and disgust with life. On the other hand, Narlikar women group telephoned him twice a day and persuaded him to sell his portion of the estate. The combined psychological pressure of solitariness, anger, grief and fear caused Ahmed Sinai a severe heart attack. Amina Sinai received a telegram from Alice in Bombay that her husband Ahmed Sinai suffered a massive heart attack. After reading the telegram, she burst into tears and said, 'Children, we're going home!' (279). Saleem was delighted that he would be back to Bombay, the city of his birth. Amina returned to Bombay with her children, Saleem and Brass Monkey and rushed to the hospital to see her ailing husband. At the sight of Ahmed Sinai, Amina miraculously regained her youth and set about the recovery and cure of her husband. She had nursed him day and night pouring her strength into his body. Her love had its reward. Ahmed was fully cured and he returned to a better self which was 'filled with contrition and forgiveness and laughter and...the finest miracle of all...love' (297). Ahmed Sinai had fallen in love with his much-maligned wife. While in the family front, peace replaced war, in the national level war took precedence over peace. Border disputes between India and China turned into a full-fledged war. On October 9, 1962 Indian army marched towards the battlefield and Saleem convened a meeting of the Midnight's Children who assembled in the parliament of his brain. While the Indian army made an 'all out effort' (298) to resist the Chinese aggression, Saleem made an all out attempt at unity among the children by burying the differences of race, colour or tongue. China's unprovoked attack on India on India on October 15, 1962 and the defeat of the Indian forces at Jhag-La-ridge coincided with the children launching a concerted assault on Saleem. They accused him of 'secrecy, prevarication, highhandedness, egotism' (298). The parliament of his brain became the battle-ground and Saleem was defenceless against the aggression of the midnight's children. He was defeated like the Indian soldiers who ran away from the advancing Chinese army. The Conference of the Midnight's Children fell apart because of internal divisiveness and dissension. It was Shiva whom Saleem denied the birthright, continued to influence the course of history to which he, like Saleem, was connected by virtue of birth at the stroke of midnight hour.

The defeat of the Indian forces at Jhag-La-ridge triggered off public optimism in the country. Meanwhile, Saleem was afflicted by an inflammation of the sinuses, a disease of congestion in the nasal passages. The nation was puffed up with optimism and the Indian parliamentarians poured out optimistic speeches against Chinese aggression and the blood of the martyrs, Saleem's sinuses swelled to block his nasal passages and the air 'thickened by optimism refused to enter his lungs' (299). In the first week of November, Indian troops renewed their attack on the Chinese and Saleem's sinuses refused to respond to medication. Indian troops were finally defeated by the Chinese on 20 November. This defeat drained the public morale and ended the optimism disease. Next morning the Chinese unilaterally declared ceasefire. Saleem was admitted to a hospital where the doctors subjected him to an operation and removed his inflamed sinuses to clear the nasal passages. This operation of the nose deprived him of his nose—given gift of telepathy and severed his connection with the children of the midnight. He stopped hearing 'Voices.' His head was now filled with the silence of the desert.

Saleem Sinai, the victim of history, became now the victim of his name. The title 'Sinai' suggests not only Mount Sinai, the place of revelation, but also it suggests 'the name of the desert—of barrenness, infertility, dust, the name of the end' (305). War with China ended showing Nehru's 'Panch Sheel' in poor light. After ceasefire and drainage, Amina and Ahmed Sinai decided to emigrate to Pakistan to make a fresh start. They sold their Buckingham Villa to the Narlikar women in February 1963 and left India for the 'Land of the pure'. Before they left, Saleem put the relics of the past, Prime Minister's letter and the *Times of India* baby snap into a battered tin globe and buried it for posterity. Soon after his arrival in Karachi, Saleem's loss of telepathy was compensated by his possession of a strong sense of smell.

JAMILA SINGER

The Sinais emigrated from India to Pakistan to strike new roots in the land of the pure. At Karachi, they were offered the hospitality of Amina's elder sister Alia Aziz who was a college principal and lived alone in a large building adjacent to a mosque whose 'long accusing shadow' (308) fell on the terrace. Saleem noticed that the windowless large Karachi houses built in a uniform grotesque style on the desert endowed the inhabitants with 'only the slipperiest of grasps on reality' (308), and they were, therefore, willing to turn to their spiritual leaders for advice on what was real and what was not. To his dismay Saleem observed that Karachiites learnt 'submission' and 'acquiescence' in all the affairs of life, a life-denying fact which was depressing to him because he had been brought up in the 'highly-spiced non-conformity of Bombay' (308). Saleem could not forgive Karachi for not being Bombay. Saleem's father, however, decided to build a new home in the land of the pure. He bought a plot of land. He was for a new beginning. Purity was his ideal. Ahmed Sinai purchased a towel factory which started producing a brand of towels named after his wife, Amina. With the help of Amina Brand towels, Ahmed Sinai declared his resolve 'to make the whole world clean' (311). In the land of the pure, Saleem's parents transformed themselves into puritans. On the other hand Saleem 'tainted with Bombayness' (310) and the liberalism of his grandfather showed an inclination to impurity and thus proved himself a misfit in the land of the pure. On his sixteenth birthday, he was given a Lambretta motor-scooter by his father. Riding the city streets on his windowless vehicle, Saleem did smell the other side of the land of the pure—the impurities and squalor of life. On reaching Pakistan, he discovered that the drainage of his sinuses only endowed him with an enhanced sense of smell. Saleem's olfactory organ gave him 'knowledge but not power-over-events' (307). With his heightened sense of smell, Saleem discovered the profane odours of the city of Karachi. Notwithstanding his study of history at his aunt's college he failed to identify himself with the country of Pakistan devoid of Midnight's children and the dream which inspired them at the hour of their birth. He noticed that his fellow-students took out processions to demand a 'stricter, more Islamic society' (310). Saleem experienced a contrast between his Indian childhood full of optimism and his adolescence in Pakistan. He also gained an insight into the political reality of the act of partitioning the subcontinent into a secular democracy and a theocratic state. India offered Saleem 'an infinity of alternative realities' but Pakistan left him confused 'amid an equally infinite number of falsenessness, unrealities and lies' (326). Saleem's sister Brass Monkey, on the other hand, turned into a God fearing angel and learnt the lesson of submission to God and cleanliness. Within a very short time of her stay in the land of the pure, Saleem's sister became the most popular singer in Pakistan. She was called the 'voice of the nation' and also the 'nightingale of the faith' (313). Her parents were persuaded to allow her sing in the public. Jamila rose to stardom in no time. Ahmed Sinai, her puritan father was reluctant at first, to allow his daughter sing on the public stage. Zulfikar's friend Latif arranged for Jamila singer an all-concealing veil with a hole at the centre. Thus, Jamila was positioned behind a perforated sheet during her public appearance. Her angelic voice was dissociated from her body. Family history repeats itself. Perforated sheet syndrome re-occurs in the life of the second generation. Thus the history of the Aziz family 'became the fate of a nation' (313). Jamila sang through the hole in the perforated sheet and Pakistan fell in love with the disembodied voice. Similarly Aadam Aziz, the grandfather had fallen in love with a partly visible beauty behind the perforated sheet years ago. In course of time, Jamila became 'the new daughter of the nation' (314). Her personality on the stage did exude the rhetoric of fanatical Islamic nationalism. She was called to sing in the President house. Ayub Khan told her that her angelic voice was like 'a sword for purity' with which the Islamic state of Pakistan would 'cleanse men's souls' (315). The word 'cleansing' as uttered by the Pakistani dictator rings ironical in the background of the post-colonial political arrangement in Pakistan which is marked by the tyranny, corruption and self-seeking of the ruling class. Within a short time, people became disenchanted with military rule of Ayub. There was a rumour in the air of 'embezzled money and Swiss Bank accounts' (315). In 1964, Ayub decreed an election. The opposition parties were united under the leadership of Fatema Jinnah, the sister of the founder of Pakistan. But the election held under the nose of the army, was rigged. The supporters of the opposition party were debarred from casting their votes. The next morning, the Pakistani newspapers announced an overwhelming victory for Ayub Khan's Muslim League, 'cleansing of souls' no doubt gets reflected in the cleansing of the election machinery in an Islamic state of Pakistan where truth is manufactured to distort reality. Saleem's narrative breaks into a fairy tale and offers a critique of Islamic democracy. In a sense, Islam and democracy go ill together.

HOW SALEEM ACHIEVED PURITY

Saleem's narrative includes the Pakistani part of the family story. Grandmother Naseem Aziz arrived in Pakistan from India in mid-1964. This year is known for bitter power-struggle in Indian politics resulting from the vacuum created by the sudden death of Prime Minister Nehru. Morarji Desai and Jagjivan Ram were united in their effort to prevent the establishment of a Nehru dynasty. Lal Bahadur Shastri was the consensus candidate for prime ministership. After her arrival in Pakistan, reverend mother settled in business with her widowed daughter-in-law, Pia and purchased a petrol pump in Rawalpindi. Naseem never grieved over the death of her husband who blamed the Muslim League and despised the God-ridden country of Pakistan. In the new country, Naseem and Pia who disliked each other turned out to be good business partners. Pia attracted customers with her beautiful look and Naseem welcomed them into her glass chamber. In course of time, Naseem lost interest in her family and became pre-occupied with other people's lives. Pia, on her part retreated into her private world and started making a series of liaisons with Pakistani cricketers and army officers. Her promiscuity was a frantic attempt to resist the inevitable decay of youth and beauty. It was nothing but an act of frustration. Saleem also started a process of withdrawal from the 'diseased reality' (338) of the God-ridden country of Pakistan. Besides, his unrequited love for his sister had heavy emotional toll on his self. He succumbed to fatalism and tried to accept all that happened as inevitable. Brass Monkey began touring the country giving concerts and Saleem moved into 'private despondency' (330) and watched the disintegration of his family in the godly country which, as it appeared to him, was an act of retribution for leaving Bombay. Saleem could not forgive his father for leaving Bombay which stood for secularism and plurality. Alia Sinai, in whose house in Karachi the Sinai family stayed, could not forgive Ahmed Sinai for abandoning her and Amina; her sister for marrying her lover. Alia Sinai's frustration resulting from spinsterhood was leaked into the college curriculum and she raised a tribe of religious fanatics in the college and her home turned into an 'insane asylum' (331). Under the vindictive sigh of the spinster, the autumnal love of Ahmed and Amina turned sour. In such a situation Amina became pregnant again in her advanced age. She became fearful, shameful and superstitious. She began to receive 'visits from the specters of her past' (332). Ahmed Sinai observed the disintegration of his wife with dismay and was unnerved. His towel factory crumbled before his eyes. He relapsed into former illness of paralyzing heart-attack which 'restored him to the dribbles and giggles of his infancy' (337). His parents' flight from reality accompanied with the ruin of his family made Saleem fatalistic. Reality was too much for Saleem's parents and so they moved back into the world of make-believe. Nothing but confusion ruled Saleem's private world.

In the public sphere too, divorce between news and reality took place. State controlled Pakistani newspapers advertised progress and transparency of the national leaders; people started cursing the so-called 'green revolution' and talking about 'Swiss bank accounts' (334). The national press spoke of the improvement of Indo-Pak relations. War broke out in April 1965 between the two countries over the 'disputed territory' (335) of the Rann of Kutchh. The Pakistani army was routed in the battle of Kutchh. The war on Rann of Kutchh triggered off a full-scale war between India and Pakistan over Kashmir.

There were claims and counterclaims from both the countries in war. Both sides claimed victory. But Saleem distrusts the official version of the war which conceals the truth. Official view of the war overlooks the resultant loss of life, pangs and sufferings. He therefore presents a subjective though fantastic version of the Indo-Pak war of 1965. Saleem's alternative view nullifies the contradictory claims of the warring countries which he terms as lies and falsehood. He exposes the pretensions of the warmongers and denounces the hollow chauvinism and communalism which inform the war-propaganda. Saleem offers a private explanation of the motive of the war. 'The hidden purpose of the Indo-Pakistani war of 1965 was the elimination of my benighted family' (338).

The fragmentation of reality and disintegration of his family took a toll on Saleem who now 'sought out the oblivion of death' (341). The narrative is clothed in fantasy and describes Indian air-raids on major Pakistani cities annihilating one by one the members of Saleem's 'drained, hopeless family' (342). Naseem, Pia, Emerald and Zafar were killed by Indian bomb in Rawalpindi. Ahmed Sinai, Amina with her unborn child and Alia were killed in Karachi. Saleem escaped death but was hit at the back of his head by his mother's silver-spittoon which had been flung in the air by the blast. The bombing incident made Saleem free of his historical role. He experienced cleansing and moved back into a state of purity and innocence of his childhood. Saleem survived the war but lost his gift of memory. He lost his hair, finger, telepathy and now memory. The disintegration of his body coincides with the cracking up of the nation. For Saleem it was a retreat from initial hope and enthusiasm to premature disenchantment.

BOOK THREE

THE BUDDHA

The Indo-Pak war of 1965 left Saleem 'orphaned and purified' (345). The blow of the flying spittoon at the back of his head, robbed him of his memory. He lost the power of feeling and further, his connection with family and history. He found himself metamorphosed into a man-dog endowed with the power of smell. 'No memory, not interested in people, lives like dog' (349). The Indo-Pakistan war saw the fall of Ayub Khan. General Yahya Khan took over the charge of the country as the next President and, as usual, declared a free and fair election. The election was held in the two wings of Pakistan in 1970 and Mujib-ur-Rahman's Awami League won a massive victory defeating the People's Party of Zulfikar Ali Bhutto. As is the way of the dictators, Mujib was denied the right to form the new Government. The period saw the rise of Bengali nationalism in the East wing of Pakistan consisting mainly of Bengali speaking people. The theocratic state of Pakistan was plunged into a civil strife when Mujib 'led the East wing into secession and declared it independent as Bangladesh' (335). In the history of the subcontinent, Bangladesh war of liberation witnessed 'the biggest migration' (357) of people and worst genocide in human history. The two wings of Pakistan, separated by thousands of miles, were held together by the glue of religion. In 1971, Pakistan got disintegrated, a historic event which gave the religious bonding of a state, a lie. Bangladesh wins freedom.

Saleem was enlisted in a CUTIA unit (a she-dog unit) of Pakistani army for his exceptional power of smell. He forgot his past, his name and identity. He grew prematurely old and was called 'buddha' in Urdu, an old man. His grotesquely adult face wore an expression of calm and quietness like the ancient sage Gautama Buddha, the enlightened. He was very submissive and obeyed the orders of others. Like Buddha, Saleem learned the art of submission and became a true citizen of Pakistan. The human experience of Pak-Bengal war is evoked through Saleem's traveling in war-ravaged East Bengal as a man dog. He saw and witnessed the atrocities committed by Pakistani forces in East Pakistan.

March 25, 1971 remains an important day in history. It was the day when Mujib-ur-Rahman proclaimed the birth of a new nation. Yahya Khan, the President sent large troops to the East Wing to quell the rebellion. Sixty thousand Pak soldiers swung into action at Midnight. The dog soldiers were released to hunt the Awami League supporters and the volunteers of the Mukti Bahini (Liberation army of Bangladesh). Saleem, the tracker of the canine unit sniffed out Mujib from his hide-out. The leader of the nationalist movement was 'manacled, manhandled' (356) and flown to West Pakistan where he was put into prison. The narrative presents a realistic detail of the horror of the fratricidal war. While riding through the streets of Dhaka, Saleem, the buddha witnessed the inhuman acts of savagery of the Pak army. Ladies were dragged out of the hostels and raped. Students, teachers, poets and journalists were either killed or arrested. Newspaper offices and factories were ransacked and burnt. 'Soldiers for Allah' (357) perpetrated a dreadful crime against humanity in an effort to hold the land of the pure united. Countryside was littered with traces of Pak-army's atrocity, burnt out villages, abandoned paddy fields, uprooted railways and large scale migration of villagers. Lastly the plundering troops advanced towards the 'darker heart of madness' (358) to the Gangetic belt of the south. Saleem took the opportunity and along with three soldiers of his unit entered the Sundarbans in a boat, 'hungry, unslept, exhausted' (358). The pre-historic rain forest situated beyond time and space, engulfed the man-dog and the three boy-soldiers.

IN THE SUNDARBANS

Saleem's narrative presents an imaginary dream forest which occupies the same geographical space as the real Sundarbans. The story moves on parallel lines of space and time. Saleem, the man dog deserted the Pakistani army by rowing a boat across southern rivers and fled to the forests of the Sundarbans for personal safety along with three boy-soldiers. It was a journey from the brutal battlefield of East Pakistan into the 'historyless anonymity' (360) of the impenetrable jungle of a geographical space called the Sundarbans. On an imaginary plane, Saleem's withdrawal into the forests of the Sundarbans was like a descent into hell. In other words, it was like entering the subconscious which the rainforest externalized. It was in the rainforest of the Sundarbans that the intruders, Saleem and three boy-soldiers could recognize their crime and met with punishment. The infernal jungle tormented them for their sins. The ordeal of suffering was not only painful but chastening too which led them to a 'new adulthood' (364).

Once Saleem and the three boy-soldiers made a forced entry into the greenness of the Sundarbans, the forest closed behind them 'like a tomb' and the boys lost their way in its 'sepulchral greenness' (360). Then the rain came which only deepened the mystery of the jungle and the surreality of the trees. In the torrential downpour, the surreal forest grew 'in size, power and ferocity' (361). The Sundari trees and the Nipa palm trees appeared to grow immensely in height so as to block out the sun. The boys rowed their boat to the shore and in a 'miasmatic state of mind' (362) fell asleep. They awoke from sleep only to find their bodies covered with blood-filled leeches. They felt hunger and thirst and drank rainwater pouring off the leaves and 'fell deeper...into the thralldom of the livid green world' (362). They built a make shift shelter with palm branches and ate Nipa fruits in their jungle life. It was a jungle beyond time where days dissolved into each other 'under the force of the returning rain' (363). Further, it was a state of primitive level of existence infested with snakes, fevers and diarrhoea. The fantastic forest whispered unpleasant secrets in their ears and punished the intruder soldiers by sending 'terrible phantasms' at night: 'the accusing eyes of the wives of men they had tracked down and seized, the screaming and monkey-gibbering of children left fatherless by their work' (363). In the elemental jungle of the Sundarbans, the boy soldiers found themselves imprisoned in retribution for their crimes. They were compelled to own up the misdeeds they had committed. The nocturnal punishment reduced the boys to their former selves until they began regressing into childhood. A snake-bite miraculously brought back buddha's memory. Words came pouring out through the lips of the enlightened (Saleem) while the rain continued pouring relentlessly and water level rose dangerously high. Saleem, the buddha and the three boy-soldiers moved deeper in the dense jungle in search of higher ground. The dense forest renewed its punishment and filled their ears with the 'accusing, pain-filled voices' (356) of their victims. Unable to bear the voices telling their 'burden of shame' (365), the boy soldiers plugged their ears with mud and turned deaf. The voices stopped their whisper and the magical forest offered the 'panic-stricken travellers' a vision. They saw an enormous Hindu temple with erotic pictures of men and women carved on its walls. They also saw inside 'towering statue of a black dancing Goddess' (366). The exhausted wanderers lay down at the feet of the Goddess Kali and fell into a sleep. While they awoke at midnight, they found four beautiful girls smiling upon them. The boys, as if in a state of hallucination, met the 'women of their most contented dreams' (367) below the statue of the black Goddess and realized that 'they were leaving infancy behind for ever' (367). The inferno of the jungle punished them for their misdeeds and now the paradise fulfilled their hearts' desire. A tidal wave threw them out of the illusive forest and they returned to the world governed by time and history. It was October 1971 and thc war at Bangladesh was nearing an end. The Mukti Bahini (the liberation army of Bangladesh) did wage the last battle against the Pakistani occupation army with the help of the Indian armed forces. The deserters rejoined the army unit. They reached Dhaka on stolen bicycles and were informed of the arrival of Indian army to liberate Bangladesh. Buddha heard someone calling him from a pyramid of mutilated bodies and found Sonny Ibrahim, his boyhood friend. The bizarre re-union with his childhood friend in the strangest of places convinced Saleem of the truth of the Bangladesh war, that the 'purpose of that entire war had been to re-unite me with an old life, to bring me back together with my old friends.' Sam Manekshaw marched to Dhaka to meet his old friend the Tiger and thus the modes of connection lingered on, actively and passively, literarily and metaphorically. In Dhaka Saleem met yet another gifted child of the midnight, Parvati-the-witch.

SAM AND THE TIGER

On December 15, 1971, in the capital city of the newly independent Bangladesh, Tiger Niazi surrendered to his old chum Sam Manekshaw, with ninety-three thousand troops. This is once again an item of historical inaccuracy. Niazi, the Pakistani General surrendered to Jagjit Singh Aurora, his Indian counterpart and not to Sam Manekshaw, the Chief of Indian army. Saleem, on his part, surrendered to the embraces of Parvati-the-witch who was also a child of the midnight and born with the gift of sorcery.

On the night of December 14, the buddha (Saleem) and Shaheed, his companion, secretly entered the beleaguered city of Dhaka and saw the instances of atrocity committed by the Pakistani troops. Innocent civilians were killed and there were mass graves; killing of the intelligentsia and the beastly torture on women proved beyond doubt, the hideous and inhuman violence perpetrated by the Pakistani army in Bangladesh in the name of holy war against the fellow brethren. The acts of violence, all around, agonized both, Buddha and Shaheed and they were apprehensive of their own safety. Buddha entered an abandoned house and found a cloak lying on a small landing. He changed his she-dog badge and turned 'anonymous' (376) in the unfamiliar city. While Shaheed was watching the goings on in the city, he was hit by a grenade explosion which blew away his leg. It was night and buddha carried away the tattered body of Shaheed to a minaret of a nearby mosque and began to wait for the day break. Buddha was shocked and complained of the unfairness of the affairs of life and the misfortune that befell his young companion. Shaheed 'screamed out the terrible agony of war' (377) through the suddenly activated loudspeaker of the minaret. He became a martyr in an insane war which relegated humans to the level of the beast. Buddha feared detection and left the mosque and joined the procession of people marching towards the centre of the city to see the ignominious surrender of the Pakistani soldiers under Niazi. There was widespread jubilation among the people of Bangladesh when the Indian army marched into the capital of the newly liberated country. Major Shiva was among the Indian war-heroes who earned fame by destroying the enemies. A large number of Indian magicians and entertainers were there in the victory march who relieved the pain of the people by wonderful display of their performances. Picture Singh, the snake charmer and Parvati-the-witch, the midnight's child born with the gift of sorcery, were there among the entertainers who delighted the people most. Parvati recognized Saleem who was in the crowd and was highly pleased with her re-union with the greatest of the midnight's children. She would not let Saleem go. While General Niazi and his troops surrendered to the Indian army and became prisoners of war, Saleem 'became the willing captive' (379) of Parvati-the-witch. She took him to India secretly hidden in a magic basket. Her magical power enabled her to make people disappear until she desired them to return. It was 'basket invisibility' which enabled Saleem to escape from Bangladesh without any passport. In the grip of Parvati's sorcery Saleem felt his hold on the world slip away and lost his power on reality. His 'prophesied historical role' (382) began to fade. What he held on in his flight in the cloud was a silver spittoon which reminded him of the outside world. He was filled with rage against the event of his birth which had linked him with the fate of his nation. 'Why, alone of all the more than five hundred million, should I have to bear the burden of history?' (382). His fury and rebellion had rescued him from the state of numbness. He was released from Parvati's magic basket and found himself on the dirt of magician's ghetto in Delhi, silver-spittoon in hand. Saleem realized that he had once again, begun to feel.

THE SHADOW OF THE MOSQUE

On December 16, 1971 Saleem tumbled out of Parvati's magic basket in the ghetto of magicians near Delhi's Friday Mosque. His return to India coincided with the supposed political rebirth of Mrs Indira Gandhi whose New Congress Party held a more-than-two-thirds majority in the Parliament. Consequently, Mrs Gandhi's abnormal hankering after power and dynastic aspiration became all too evident. It was such a time when, as per reports, corruption in high places was institutionalized. Mrs Gandhi showed her inclination towards astrology and occult powers. In short, the nation was moving backwards and there was a shift from Nehru's secular democratic legacy. Saleem had been overwhelmed by an agonizing feeling of sympathy for the country. He decided to save the country from the drift. He resolved to leave the Magician's ghetto and go to his only surviving uncle Mustapha Aziz in New Delhi. He understood that his uncle, an influential bureaucrat would help him fulfil his 'Messianic ambitions' (388). He also was of the opinion that with the active support of the bureaucrat, he would 'find the keys of national salvation' (389). Under the roof of the bureaucrat uncle, he would find the ears of the ministers and would be in the company of the great in the administration. Saleem was in the grip of this magnificent fantasy when Parvati told him of her encounter with Shiva in a Dacca procession. Shiva with the knees in his military uniform parading the Dacca streets was, as Saleem understood, the man of destiny. Parvati and Shiva, Shiva and Parvati, fated to meet by the 'divine destiny of their names' (395). In Dacca, they were united in the moment of victory. Saleem walked away from her to the home of Mustapha Aziz, the rich relative.

Mustapha was a senior Civil Servant and loyal to the Prime Minister. He spent his spare time filling large log-books with spider-like family trees and doing research on the lineages of the greatest families of the land. He would place his genealogical log books at the service of the Prime Minister who was 'falling increasingly beneath the twin spells of power and astrology' (392). Once Saleem saw, amongst his genealogical log books, a black leather folder labeled 'To secret' and titled 'Project M.C.C.' The narrator makes a caustic observation regarding the drift of the national politics on the road to feudalism.

> ...but while the Indira Sarkar, like her father's administration, consults daily with purveyors of occult lore, while Banarasi seers help to shape the history of India, I must digress into painful, personal recollections; because it was at Uncle Mustapha's that I learned, for certain, about the deaths of my family in the war of' 65 (394).

Saleem learned that his sister Jamila, the Voice of Pakistan, Bulbul of the faith, had spoken out against the rulers of the war-divided Pakistan and had disappeared from the face of the earth. Saleem spent the next four hundred and twenty days in belated mourning for the dead. His dream of preferment in public service during his stay with the bureaucrat uncle evaporated in no time as he found that Mustapha nourished a canine devotion to Indira Gandhi and the power that be. He lost faith in spineless bureaucrat and returned to the Magicians slum, his 'true inheritance of poverty and destitution' (396), and found shelter in the shadow of the Friday mosque. Like Gautama, the first and true Buddha, he left his life of comfort at the bureaucrat's house and went like a beggar into the world. The shadow of the mosque offered him relief from the heat of the sun. He felt comfortable in the slum and could endure cold, hunger and thirst. There developed solidarity between him and the Magicians who were Communists. Picture Singh, the communist snake charmer was the Leader of the slum. He spoke of socialism which owed nothing to foreign influences. In spite of poverty and ills of life the slum dwellers were subjected to, the ghetto was free from 'religious and regionalist bigotry' (399). Picture Singh was the patriarch of the ghetto. He possessed an umbrella whose shade did restore harmony to the squabbling factions. Saleem shared the shack of Picture Singh and fell under his spell. He was again filled with an optimism because the Communist Picture Singh offered him an alternative vision of things. It was Picture Singh who initiated Saleem into politics and revealed to him the corrupt 'black' economy and white economy. He showed a photograph of Mrs Gandhi showing her hair-style, her hair parted in the centre, was snow-white on one side and black as night on the other.

But the patriarch of the slum was not without a heart. He loved the fatherless girl of the slum, Parvati-the-witch like his own daughter. He began to search for a husband for her. He requested Saleem to marry the gifted daughter of the midnight. But Saleem turned down the proposal. He could not marry her because he was cursed with impotence.

A WEDDING

Saleem refused to marry Parvati-the-witch who helped him to escape from East Pakistan. Spurned by Saleem, Parvati remembered his arch-enemy Shiva. She called to Shiva and Shiva came. At the end of the war in East Pakistan, Shiva had risen to 'Commanding heights' (407) and Saleem fell and became a penniless slum-dweller. The war of 1971 turned Shiva into a national idol. The legends of his exploits in the Pakistani war constituted the front lines in the national newspapers and he found himself elevated in social status as well as in military rank. He was invited to innumerable social gatherings 'to be applauded and monopolized by the noblest and the fairest' (407). The beautiful wives of the rich and the powerful were attracted to the charismatic army officer and fell into his arms. Shiva became a notorious seducer and fathered innumerable bastards on the women and wives across the country. He had nourished hatred and ill-will for the nobility and the rich and had a 'desire to be done with the rich bitches of Indian high society' (410). It was at this time that Parvati remembered him through her magic spell. He did recall his meeting her in Dacca and went to see her in the ghetto of magicians on 18 May 1974. The meeting of Shiva and Parvati was fraught with grave consequences as it was in the same year the desert of Pokhran was rocked by India's first nuclear explosion. Saleem's lie drove Parvati to the arms of his arch-rival, who is Wee Willie Winkie's boy Shiva. Throughout his narrative, Saleem pushed Shiva into the background. There are ironies in the turn of events. 'Had not Shiva risen as Saleem fell' (423). Parvati left the colony and went with Shiva to the army quarters. She turned the simple army quarters into a palace, a Kailasa fit for Shiva the God and Major Shiva devoted his attention to her for four months. On September 12, Parvati, kneeling at his feet told Shiva that she was going to have his child.

This revelation only turned the Shiva-Parvati relation into a stormy business. Shiva had the habit of losing interest in pregnant women and deserted them when they became pregnant. Fights and quarrels ensued and Shiva and Parvati liaison became an earthly echo of the marital battle of the Gods which their namesakes are reported to perform on Mount Kailasa in the Great Himalayas. Shiva was full of fury and anger at Parvati's disclosure and began drinking and whoring all over the country. At this time Indian people were getting angry with the corrupt Government of Indira Gandhi. By the end of 1974, Socialist leaders like Jaya Prakash Narayan and Gandhian leader Morarji Desai formed a coalition of opposition parties known as Janata Morcha against the ruling Indira Congress. On a cold morning in 1975 Railway Minister L.N. Misra was killed by an explosion. Shiva dragged Parvati by the hair and left her in the slum. On the other hand, Saleem became disillusioned with the Communists and their leader in the ghetto, Picture Singh. He realized that his dream of national salvation was 'insubstantial, the maundering of a fool' (413). People of the slum were not happy at the return of Parvati with a child in her womb and they hurled abuses at her. Picture Singh again requested Saleem to marry her and save her honour like in the past when she saved her life in violence-ridden East Pakistan. On the republic Day of 1975, Saleem married Parvati-the-witch who bore Shiva's child. Saleem's wife Parvati was converted to Islam and she took a new name, Laylah. Like his mother Amina, Parvati changed her name because she would give birth to a child who would be born to a father not his own. The birth of Saleem's child mirrored Saleem's own because the birth of the child coincided with the declaration of Emergency on the midnight of 25 June, 1975.

On June 12, Prime Minister Indira Gandhi was found guilty by Allahabad High Court of malpractice during the election campaign of 1971 and it was precisely at 2 p.m. Parvati had entered labour. The labour lasted for thirteen days, the period which coincided with the political turmoil in the country consequent upon Mrs Gandhi's refusal to resign after the court verdict. The midwives in the labour room urged Parvati to push and push, the opposition leaders urging Indira to resign and thus forcing her to deliver a child of her own. On the stroke of midnight, 25 June, 1975 Indira Gandhi proclaimed Emergency and suspended civil rights. At that 'precise instant of the birth of the new India' (419), Saleem's son Aadam Sinai was born. He was born with flapping ears like those of an elephant as her father Saleem was born with elephantine nose. The child of the Emergency refused to cry. Its birth at the darkest hour marked the end of the Nehruvian era of democracy and the country's arrival at Emergency. The mute baby thus, at birth, like his adoptive father, became 'handcuffed to history' (420). The boy Aadam Sinai also was the child of his time which was out of joint.

MIDNIGHT

Aadam Sinai, Saleem's child born at the precise hour of another midnight in 1975 was infected with tuberculosis and did not respond to medical treatment. The disease was 'darkly metaphorical' (422) and was not cured until the dark period of Emergency was over. The child born at the precise hours of Emergency was mute and did not cry. The speechlessness of the infant signified the fear of the people under the dark days of Emergency and the lack of freedom of speech. Both the father and the son are born 'handcuffed to history' but while Saleem, the child of the midnight hour of independence fell a victim to the 'joint tyrannies of family and fate', his son Aadam, the child of Emergency 'fought ferociously, refusing to yield' (425). He was tougher and stronger than his father. Emergency signified the dark period in the history of the country and Saleem's son showed signs of stunted growth. The fact that the child did not respond to medication made his mother sad. Parvati had suffered from a feeling of despair because of her unconsummated love and marriage. Saleem could not share her bed and he had no solace to offer to his bereaved wife. While the Government of India changed the Constitution of the country and gave the Prime Minister 'absolute powers' (424) Saleem smelt 'the sharp aroma of despotism' (424) which had descended on the body politic. He became worried about his own life and the safety of the Midnight's Children. The Communist snake-charmer was old and the slum dwellers were apprehensive. In the wake of Emergency, a gloomy silence had descended on the slum. Incredible things happened in Delhi and throughout the country. Here and there people vanished inexplicably and slums and ghettos mysteriously disappeared from the face of the earth.

The state controlled media deified the Prime Minister Indira Gandhi and equated her with the nation. The fascist slogans like 'Indira is India and India is Indira' rang in the air. Nameless fear gripped the minds of the people who remained silent spectators about the crimes and atrocities of the dictatorial government. Truth, reality and news were doctored by the censored press. Tyrannical forces were let loose to discipline the people and also to crush all opposition to the Prime Minister. Indira Gandhi became synonymous with 'Bharat Mata.' Many self-seekers and opportunists gathered around her and Major Shiva was one of them. He became Indira's henchman and 'a warlord of tyranny' (430). The Emergency meant forced uniformity and conformity. Dissenting opinions and multiplicity of views were ruthlessly suppressed. The Midnight's children were different and hence they constituted a threat to the unitary world-view of the dictatorial authority. Consequently, Indira Gandhi found in Saleem a rival whose self-delusion of representing the multiple India ran counter with the authoritarianism of the Prime Minister. The turn of events in the national politics constitutes an irony of the birth of the greatest child of the midnight upon whom the late Prime Minister Jawaharlal Nehru bestowed 'the role of the mirror of the nation' through a letter in which 'her own, sloganized centrality was denied' (427). The star-obsessed widow prime minister could learn about the presence of the Midnight's children through her astrologers and was bent upon destroying them as they were opposed to her idea of conformity and consensus. Saleem became convinced that the purpose behind the declaration of emergency was the liquidation of the miraculous children who stood for an alternative reality of multiplicity and plurality. On a winter morning a group of volunteers of Sanjay Gandhi's Youth Congress did arrive at the magicians' slum with medical vans and bulldozers with the double purpose of civic beautification programme and forced sterilization. The slum dwellers put up a resistance under the leadership of Picture Singh but their resistance was of no avail. Major Shiva and his troops opened fire on the slum dwellers and bulldozed their hovels and homes. Parvati was killed in the turmoil and Saleem started running away leaving behind his son. But he was pursued, captured and was betrayed by his arch-enemy Shiva who had come to the slum upon the instruction of the widow, to arrest Saleem, the man 'who held the key to the location of every single one of the children of the midnight' (432). Saleem was taken to Benares and forced to betray his midnight siblings. A massive hunt was conducted throughout the country to round them up. Midnight's children were caught and brought to the widow's hostel and tortured. Saleem 'gave way to his grief' (434). He was disillusioned. Indira Gandhi feared the magical children and planned their extermination because she found in their existence a challenge to her supremacy. For the next eighteen days the children of independent India were taken to underground chambers and 'vas-and-tubectomized' by doctors and their 'ectomized parts' (440) were fried and fed to the pie dogs. The children represented the 'one thousand and one marvelous promises of a numinous midnight' as Saleem understood philosophically. 'Who were we? Broken promises' (439). Because of compelling circumstances, Emergency was lifted in the middle of January and in the following election Indira Gandhi's party was defeated. The Janata Party came to power under the leadership of the Morarji Desai. In March, political prisoners including the children of midnight were released from captivity. The traumatic experience of Emergency only unnerved Saleem. He was disillusioned with post-colonial politics altogether and lost his connection with history and politics. He was drained of all hope in a new dawn and made his way back to Delhi with the knowledge that the new age which had begun on the Midnight of 15th August 1947 amidst promises and possibilities came to an end.

ABRACADABRA

Post Emergency period in the history of the country saw Saleem reduced from the status of the protagonist at the centre to the victim in the periphery. Castrated by the widow, he was now prematurely old 'to whom history could do no more' (477). Dark days of Emergency haunted the memory of the people in the changed dispensation under the Janata Party rule. Aadam had been cured of tuberculosis with the end of the Emergency. Communist musicians stopped talking about social change and the rule of the proletariat. After his return from captivity, Saleem found no reason to stay alive but his child demanded care and attention and he was compelled to live. Aadam was of only two years of age but was tough and strong-willed kid. The 'mute autocracy' of the child was a pointer to the fact that he 'was a member of a second generation of magical children who would grow far tougher than the first' and they would frame their fate 'in the implacable furnaces of their wills' (447). Notwithstanding the fact that Emergency had destroyed the thousand and one new hopes and promises of the newly independent nation, thousand strong-willed sons including Aadam Sinai, Shiva's bastards, represented to Saleem, the nation's hope for regeneration. There was optimism in the birth of Aadam, Saleem's son who was born of the union of Shiva and Parvati who represent the most powerful God and Goddess and the mythical cycle of destruction and regeneration. The first word that Aadam Sinai uttered was 'abracadabra' a symbolic word which indicated the inheritance of Parvati, the mother.

Saleem reaches the end of his autobiography in words and pickles. The narrative ends with Saleem's impotence and imminent disintegration. With the decline of the hopes and thousand possibilities of 15th August '47, Saleem whose life mirrored the fate of the nation, started cracking up at an alarming rate. Hence the narrator is in a hurry to recollect and record his experiences. He also tries to impose an order and meaning on chaotic life experience through writing and pickling. He understands that there is distortion of the pickling process as there is unreliability regarding his record of history. But then Saleem the narrator and the authorial alter-ego is not obsessed with purity. 'To pickle is to give immortality.' Saleem now drained of his power, watches his countrymen preparing to celebrate the coming Independence Day which coincides with his thirty-first birth day. He feels in the air a note of cynism, despair and a sense of waste. The myth of a modern nation born thirty years ago on the midnight of 15th August has faded into memory. Post-colonial India requires new myths to inspire the people and the task is left to the new generation of Shiva and Parvati's bastard offsprings. Saleem is not obsessed with purity.

His own generation of the Midnight's children has been cursed 'to be both masters and victims of their times...and...sucked into the annihilating whirlpool of the multitudes...to be unable to live or die in peace' (463). Destruction and regeneration—the wheel of the story comes full circle.

3

Major Themes and Issues

'To understand just one life, you have to swallow the world' (109), so observes the narrator Saleem in Salman Rushdie's epic novel *Midnight's Children* (1981). In this text, the narrator hero is philosophically obsessed with a desire, rather Indian desire, for the whole. He attempts to swallow all of India. This desire for the whole, the multitude may be understood as a veritable Indian disease. Noted critic Srivastava sees this desire 'as a specifically Indian urge to encapsulate the whole of reality' (Srivastava 62). Therein lies Saleem's ambition and downfall.

Salman Rushdie's second novel *Midnight's Children* published in 1981 was hailed as a 'Post-colonial meta-fiction, a novel about third world novels' (Brennan 85). Since 80s, a wave of novels by Indian English writers appeared that were clearly influenced by this seminal Rushdie text and its conception of national literature. Rushdie's examination of the relationship between the self and the nation, and his advocacy of the concept that there are as many equally valid version of the truth as there are Indians, proved liberating for the Indian English writers. *Midnight's Children* has been the major post-colonial novel in English which fictionalizes the events of Indian history from the moment of the birth of nation state in 1947 till the declaration of the emergency by the Congress Prime Minister Indira Gandhi in 1976 which did a death knell to the monolithic dream of a secular-democratic nation-state, perhaps insufficiently imagined, and expressed in the midnight speech by the first Prime Minister. Dreams of the founding fathers since '60s turned into a veritable myth and writers expressed disillusionment with the corruption and failure of the nation-state. In opposition to the monolithic concept of the nation, of the history, *Midnight's Children* advocates plurality of our fractured selves. The narrative is determined from the outside, by a pretext of the epical myths, orality and religion.

Role of Ancient Myths, Fantasy and Orality in Explaining Contemporary History

Notwithstanding their absolute involvement in history, their individuality, the narrator in a Rushdie text are, more often than not, fantastic and yet are real. Rushdie returned to India in the late '70s as a young man of 30 in the aftermath of emergency when many Indians expressed outrage at the Congress party's betrayal of the secular-democratic ideals on which the early post-independence generation had been raised. In *Midnight's Children*, Rushdie re-affirms and seeks to re-create, in a post modernist way, the lost nationalistic democratic ideals for the underdog and the under-privileged. Post-colonial history thus reproduced is fictionalized and mythicized.

Saleem, the principal narrator, the most gifted of 1001 Midnight's children, has been endowed with a magical power and a vision. His physical impotence and deformed shape may be read as a caricature of the political map of India. All the midnight's children are born with special power, with hundred and thousand possibilities but all these possibilities are simply wasted. Saleem and Shiva are born with contrasting qualities. They are leaders of the group but they have their double, one in reality and another in the realms of myth. Saleem stands for the whole, abundance. He contains within him the mythical creator Brahma. Shiva is the god of destruction and hence, is a rival to Saleem. The novel remains as allegory of Indian history and may be read as a literature of subversion of every form of convention and authority. The narrator patterns his own storytelling on oral narration and deploys fantasy in order to be faithful to the reality of India, a country and a nation where millions believe in the world of Spirits. In *Midnight's Children* Rushdie presents an ideological post-colonial critique of the linear, imperialist discourse of meta-history which represses rather distorts India's own account of history.

India is a vast and ancient land teeming with millions of people of different races and colours. Ancient epics, myths and oral tradition inform the lives of the people even today. The elephant headed Ganesh is the great storyteller in the ancient epic, the *Mahabharata*. He is the patron-deity of arts and literature. In *Midnight's Children*, Saleem, the powerful narrator is portrayed as a storyteller of Ganesh like skill. He is born with elephantine nose while his alter ego Shiva is all knees. Saleem is a reporter of the events of history, he creates alternative history by creating things out of memory and imagines truth as opposed to the truth of history. He preserves his materials in the chutney of fantasy and myth (pickling process). At day time he works in the chutney factory and during night he writes his stories for the imagined listener Padma (Lotus). Lotus has an association with mud. Padma likes listening stories of sensation and thrill. She has no power of intellection and thought. She believes in stories and more stories. Indian subaltern multitude is gullible and is swayed by the rhetoric of the politicians and vote catchers easily. Saleem has the potential of an omniscient and omnipotent narrator; creator as well as preserver. He is modern Vishnu. Empowering himself in mythology, the all knowing narrator chutnifies his own version of history and truth. It is "memory's truth, because memory has its own special kind. It selects, eliminates, alters, exaggerates, minimizes, glorifies and vilifies also: but in the end, it creates its own reality" (*MC* 253).

Entire narrative is clothed in fantasy. Myth and reality overlap boundaries. Fantasy may be seen as seriously narrating political reality when the readers are the author share certain views. In this novel, numerical exactitude is a feature which relates fact to fantasy. In his 1983 interview, Rushdie states his fascination for figures when he said, 'It seemed to me that the period between 1947 and 1977 the period from independence to emergency had a kind of shape to it. It represented a sort of close period in the history of the country. That shape became part of the architecture of the work' (Interview with Salman Rushdie by C. Pattanayak 1983).

Saleem's narrative is valuable precisely because it is self-conscious and invites judgment and criticism. He claims omnipotence and omniscience as a narrator, but more often than not, he laments his inability, his lack, his impotence. There is a kind of post-modern playfulness and trivialization which inform Saleem's narrative and which instills in the mind faith, doubt or questioning. Why and how should the alternative to Saleem be Shiva, a figure of violence? What is the lesson of emergency? If the idea of a secular nation-state and history be rejected, would the rule of anarchy and lawlessness descend on the life of the nation? Shiva represents the dispossessed without a stake in the dream of the nation and constitutes a political threat to Saleem's plural India. Shiva, very like his mythical origin, is made to signify chaos and unmeaning. He, in the text becomes Indira Gandhi's henchman during the Emergency when the sterilization of Midnight's Children metaphorically nullifies the hope and possibilities with which they were born. Only he, Shiva, escapes the bulldozer and thus fathers the next generation. There is a glimmer of hope in the end that Saleem can claim one of Shiva's offspring as his own son. He thus becomes able to write his autobiography for his son, the elephant-eared son born of Shiva and Parvati, Saleem's wife. Thus Saleem is not the biological father of his own son, just as he himself is not the biological son of Amina Sinai and Ahmed Sinai, his foster parents. But then the theme of illegitimate birth can be traced back to the grand epic *Mahabharata*. Is it not the fact that the mythical god of Ganesh, the god of fortune, Karna and many other mythical figures are bastards? In *Midnight's Children*, the theme of illegitimacy perhaps constitutes a critique of the concept of the purity of race, class and nation and may be seen as an item of criticism of the concept of Hindutwa *vis-à-vis* the concept of multiculturalism which may adequately explain Indian nationalism. Narrator Saleem is born of Vanita, a Hindu wife of a magician singer, by an Englishman, Methwold and nourished by Muslim parents, that too, because of a magical act of the exchange of children at birth in the hospital. Thus, he is allowed to be bathed in the confluence of world religions, Hinduism, Islam and Christianity. Metaphorically the narrator is endowed with plural identities and stands for post-colonial India.

In his personal heritage, the identity of the country emerges. His birth coincides with the birth of a modern nation, nay two nations and subsequently three (Bangladesh). Birth of the narrator and the birth of the nation take place precisely at the same hour thus at birth Saleem is 'handcuffed to History.' He is the child of history as other Midnight's children are. He grows, develops and finally goes into cracks and fragments in the same way as the nation grows and develops and experiences fissures in the body politic. This interplay of the personal and national histories gives the narrative shape and a sense of unity to the novel. This metaphoric consciousness of history, awareness of oneself as a blend of past and present, makes the narrator Saleem realize that history operates on a grander scale than any individual.

"Who, what am I? My answer: I am the sum total of everything that went before me, of all I have seen been done, of everything done to me. I am everyone everything whose being-in-the-world affected was affected by mine. I am anything that happens after I've gone which would not have happened if I had not come." (*MC* 457).

Critique of the Concept of Post-colonial Nationalism *vis-à-vis* Indian Writing in English

Rushdie once referred to Indian English writing as 'Empire's bastard child' (Rushdie talk 4-4-1997). Is not Saleem, the principal narrator of the same status? In *Midnight's Children*, the chief protagonist Saleem can be seen as an indication Indian writing in English claiming centrality of position. But by now, English language has achieved centrality by virtue of the fact that among other things Rushdie, as a technician, has made it the fit medium for conveying indigenous consciousness. Rushdie's position as a man and as a writer needs to be understood in this context. He lays claim to India, a kind of centrality and also a sense of engagement with the history of the subcontinent. He like his hero Saleem Sinai has been 'handcuffed to history' in a special sense. He was born in June 1947 and two months after, the British left India.

Midnight's Children portrays the delirious joy of the people which accompanies the formal dissolution of the empire and birth of Indian nation-state at the precise hour of the midnight in 1947 when Mountbatten hands over power to Nehru, the first Prime Minister. Nehru's famous midnight speech coined in the finest English language sounds metaphoric and ironic.

> '...years ago we made a tryst with destiny.... A moment comes, which comes but rarely when the soul of a nation long suppressed finds utterance...'

the sub-text of this metaphoric speech turns out to be a text of collaboration with the English educated nationalist elite. The leaders of the new state will, no doubt reproduce the colonial method of control and exploitation. It becomes the story of a new nation, 'insufficiently imagined.' Chances of forging a new nationalist discourse are simply lost sight of, as the subsequent happenings will prove. The Raj leaves behind hollow men like Ahmed Sinai. Methwold's transfer of property to indigenous elite like Ahmed Sinai, who ape an Oxford drawl land who are secretly pleased when they lose pigmentation due to skin-disease, because it makes them resemble the Europeans, is an eloquent testimony to the nature of independence. This tendency still persists with our academicians and professionals. Colonial institutions still have surprising spell over our mind. It is resolved that Methwold Estate is to be preserved and retained. Saleem describes the estate thus, 'Methwold's Estate: four identical houses built in a style befitting their original residents—large durable mansions with red gabled roofs and turret towers in each corner, ivory-white corners towers wearing pointy red-tiled hats...houses which their owner, William Methwold had named majestically after the palaces of Europe' (*MC* 94).

This allegorical statement by the narrator suggests the passing on of the colonial mantle to the Indian nationalist elite which not only inherited power from the colonial masters but also love for the exotic as opposed to the indigenous. In the new dispensation progress means back-pedaling, rise of fanaticism and the cracking up of Indian independence. 'India had been divided anew. But the boundaries of these states were not formed by rivers or mountains or any natural features of the terrain: they were instead walls of words. Language divided us' (*MC* 189). In the same process the subcontinent was divided. The departing imperialist did a parting kick by dividing the subcontinent on religious lines and installing a class of people who would carry Macaulay's legacy—brown in skin and English in character. Eloquent Nehru and Ahmed Sinai belong to this class. *Midnight's Children* thus constitutes a critique of nationalist rhetoric which makes a linear downward journey from 1947 to 77, the year of the declaration of national Emergency which means the curtailment of democratic rights of the people. The episode of the emergency and Mrs Gandhi is described as an allegory which is an indictment of the state controlled media. The media projects the dictator as god and Mrs Gandhi as Devi, the mother Goddess in her terrible aspect with a centre-parting hair. The fascist slogan 'Indira is India' (*MC* 427) is relayed over the media. The Nehruvian dream of secular democratic nation comes a full circle and post-emergency period sees the dethronement of the fascist god, end of one party rule and installation of a Janata Coalition government which, henceforth, becomes the shape of Indian politics. Democracy demands a plural society as opposed to unitary one.

However, despite the sense of despair, the journey from wholeness to fragments, the novel ends on a note of hope, rather political one; that is the intensification of the struggle of polarized political forces in opposition in Congress model of nationalism. As the narrative progresses, the disintegration becomes quicker and quicker, Saleem mentions cracks in his body. 'My poor body, singular, unlovely, buffeted by too much history, has started coming apart at the seams. In short I am literally disintegrating slowly for the moment.... I shall eventually crumble into six hundred and thirty million particles of anonymous and oblivious dust' (*MC* 37). With his final words the disintegrating Saleem prophesies his fate and articulates the post-colonial condition of the generation of midnight's children.

'Yes, they will trample me underfoot.... Reducing me to specks of voiceless dust...because it is the privilege and curse of the midnight's children to be both masters and victims of their times' (63). At the end, Saleem's body cracks into as many parts as there are Indians and there are as many stories to tell. Saleem has told his story, may be imperfect and unreliable but nevertheless his own. 'Stubbornly and against all odds, victim transforms himself into protagonist, simply through the telling of his own story (Rege 200).

The crisis of the Unitary nation state opens up space for thousand contending claims and it seems that the 'Crisis of the once dominant nationalism opened up space for new discursive models' (Rege 201). Thus there is a tension between the narrator and the narrative. Saleem, the narrator may sound pessimistic but the feeling of the book remains affirmative in its abundance, multiplicity and urbanism. At the impressionable age, Rushdie felt deep attachment for the urban city of his birth, the metropolitan city of Bombay for its spirit of abundance, secularism, cosmopolitanism and urban culture.

Midnight's Children as a City Novel

This epic novel was conceived in a dream about the large Indian city of Bombay, an industrial city, a city of film, and also of a young man's dream. For a long time the author had cherished a desire of writing a big and voluminous book about Bombay where he was born in June 1947. The city was in his dream because of its uniqueness, its films, cosmopolitanism and urbanity. He left Bombay for England in his teens for higher education as James Joyce left Dublin for Paris. Bombay was to Rushdie as Dublin was to Joyce. In both cases, the relationship of the artist with the city of his birth remains problematised. For a migrant writer, the concepts like home and nation are imaginary constructs. The city as a metaphor defines the authorial self and in a way informs the novel. In his collection of Essays *Imaginary Homelands*, Rushdie observes 'to be a Bombayite and afterwards a Londoner was also to fall in love with the metropolis' (*IH* 404). 'The metropolis embodies hybridity, impurity, intermingling...culture, ideas, politics, movies, songs' (*IH* 394). Post-colonial subject can find no better paradigm than the city to define his self. In the colonial times, the culture of the city was considered alien and non-pure. In the novels of Raja Rao, R.K. Narayan and others, an ideal village was considered as a true signifier of Indianness and Indian values. In Raja Rao's *The Serpent and the Rope* (1960) the hero rejects the metropolitan Indian as un-Indian.

Bombay being an industrial city had no meaning for a Brahmin like Raja Rao. Indian fiction has travelled a long way from 1960s, and in Rushdie's 1980s novel the metropolitan and industrial city of Bombay appears to be a true signifier of Indianness. Politically Indian nation state prefers the Nehruvian dream of secular and democratic modern Industrial India to "the rural handicraft-loving sometime medieval figure of Gandhi" (Attenborough's *Gandhi* 104). If the villages are considered to be the site for Indian values and if true Indianness is supposed to be constituted by Brahminical hierarchy and the purity of race and caste, modern nation has no future. Modern city is the site for plurality and multiplicity, and hence, the modern Indian villages must go the city way in respect of culture which is not unitary and plural. In its cosmopolitan nature, the city of Bombay represents an India which through the ages, has been the confluence of many nations and races, East and West. In the post-colonial situation, the terms like 'pure country' and 'corrupt city' do not exist. Post-coloniality and hybridity go together. The reading of *Midnight's Children*, a post-colonial text, in the context of other cultural production may be meaningful. We know Rushdie's focus is not the realistic portrayal of the events of post-colonial history but rather a third world consciousness of history, truth and nation shaped through myth, fantasy, dream and orality, the tools that constitute an umbrella term 'magic realim.' Bombay cinema has all along remained a site for fantasy, hallucination, dream and wish-fulfilment for the Indians irrespective of class affiliations.

The narrative of *Midnight's Children* parodies Bombay cinema's fantasy operations. Stock narrative situations like mistaken exchange at birth and stock cinema figures like good 'ayah' Mary Pereira recall Bombay film. The most frequently discussed cinematic element of *Midnight's Children* is the exchange of the infants Shiva and Saleem at birth. Rushdie himself in his essay "Midnight's Children and Shame" makes a significant comment on this particular cinematic convention.

'...This melodramatic device...was a genuine kind of Bombay Talkie, B-movie notion and I thought that a book which grew out of the movie city ought to contain such notions. These are children not so much of their parents but children of time, children of history' (Rushdie, *Midnight's Children* and *Shame* 4). Other cinematic operations are that of natural mothers who are perfect and stepmothers who are evil. Virtuous male protagonists are contrasted with evil counterparts and so on. Shiva, Saleem's alter-ego combines the role of rebel-hero with the villain of Bombay film. In 70s and 80s, the reach of Bombay cinema and its influence on Indian mind can easily be imagined. By sheer volume of production and star-charisma, Bombay film dominates the dream of the millions even in the anti-Hindi southern states. Thus Bombay film industry becomes 'an important agency for Hindi-speaking cultural hegemony in post-independence India' (Natarajan 167). Benedict Anderson's thesis about the fictional component of nation, the role of print in helping people imagine themselves as nationals along with others they have not seen, is powerfully pertinent to a consideration of cinema (with imagined communities). Thus the Bombay film, with its apparatus of myth and fantasy provides a site for mythic unity in the fact of fragmentation of the body politic in the contemporary India.

On the realistic level, such conventions suggest the plurality of post-colonial identities. Saleem represents, the multiple and complex identities of the post-colonial Indian because he is born of British father and Hindu mother, exchanged at birth by Christian nurse and brought up by Muslim businessman as his son. This comic-epic novel is a blend of literary genres and is coined in a mood of irony, satire and fantasy but the author has serious purpose in mind. The narrative is devised in a mood of playfulness, non-seriousness, trivialization as post-modern fictions mostly are. Rushdie's act of juxtaposing myth and contemporary post-colonial Indian history serves a model of intertextuality which inform among other texts, Sashi Tharoor's work *The Great Indian Novel*. But in the case of Rushdie, the classic myth only explains the contemporary situation. Tharoor trivializes the epical heroes in a mood of hilarity. Juxtaposition of trivial and serious, elitism and mass culture of Bombay film, centrally and marginality of positions and *vice versa*, purity and hybridity of racial and national identities and post-coloniality of history are the major themes and issues which the epic novel *Midnight's Children* successfully addresses.

4

Art of Characterization

Rushdie's art of characterization appears to be an attempt at defamiliarisation of the identity of his heroes and heroines. In *Midnight's Children*, Saleem Sinai is the principal character but the identity of his biological parents is held in suspense. The parents or the family has been traditionally accepted as central to a person's identity. In most of Rushdie's novels, it is seen that the characters do not really care who their parents are. In other words, they do not attach much value to the concept of the sanctity of birth or marriage. We may read in the Rushdie novels, a kind of deconstruction of identity in its traditional sense.

Saleem Sinai in *Midnight's Children* makes the reader believe that Ahmed and Amina Sinai, a wealthy Indian couple are his parents. Also, he gives a detailed description of the life and adventures of his parents. It is as if, Saleem creates or constructs his own parents in his imagination. In the middle of the novel, it becomes clear to the reader that Saleem is actually not the midnight's child Saleem Sinai, but he was exchanged at birth for Shiva, another midnight's child. After the delivery at the nursing home, the nurse Mary Pereira swapped the two babies. The reader is also informed that Saleem happens to be the child of the poor busker Wee Willie Winkie and his wife Vanita. But Vanita, nine months before the delivery, had sexual intercourse with the Englishman William Methwold and thus Saleem turns out to be of Anglo-Indian descent (*MC* 118). Saleem denies this stain on his birth and chooses to believe that Ahmed and Amina are his parents. It appears, Saleem deliberately constructs his parents and also later, names other potential parents: the nurse Mary Pereira and Nadir Khan or Picture Singh (127, 378). This multiplication of parentage in *Midnight's Children* as well as in *The Ground Beneath Her Feet* shows the protagonists as being in a state of orphanhood and displacement. Traditional view of identity states that a person's character is determined by his or her environment in which he or she grows up. But Rushdie protagonists are mostly migrants and hence the place of birth or environment has nothing to do with the shaping of the protagonist's character or personality. In *Midnight's Children* Saleem travels the entire subcontinent by his telepathic powers. The notion of fixed identity does not work and consequently the characters in a Rushdie novel are rootless, hybrids, are products of diversity and intermingling of cultures. In his essay "Imaginary Homelands," Rushdie observes,

> Our identity is at once plural and partial. Sometimes we feel that we straddle two Cultures; at other times that we fall between two stools. But however ambiguous and shifting this ground may be, it is not an infertile territory for the writer to occupy (15).

Rushdie characters create their identities by means of creating pieces of art and hence the identity is nothing but cultural constructs. In *Midnight's Children*, Saleem creates his identity by writing. 'I must work fast, faster than Scheherazade, if I am to end up meaning, yes, meaning something' (38).

Post-modern theories of subjectivity may be profitably applied in respect of Rushdie characters. Fragmentation and mutability inform the portrayal of characters in *Midnight's Children*. 'O eternal opposition of inside and outside! Because, a human being, inside himself is anything but a whole, anything but homogenous; all kinds of every which thing are jumbled up inside him, and he is one person one minute and another the next' (236-37). In a Rushdie novel, the self is divided and fragmented and hence, post-modern subjectivity is not static and fixed. Fragmentation of self is a recurring theme in Rushdie novel. Physical fragmentation works as a central metaphor for psychic fragmentation in *Midnight's Children*. Aadam Sinai's 'fragmented' views of his future bride seen through the perforated sheet at the beginning of the novel and the 'symbolic hole' inside of him (expressing Aadam's religious disbelief) are of much significance. There is further textual evidence regarding Saleem Sinai's bodily mutilation. Saleem's hair is 'torn out by a teacher' (232), a part of his middle finger is 'cut off in a struggle with other pupils about a girl' (234-35), he is 'sterilised' (439), throughout the narrative he discovers 'cracks in his body' (179). The physical mutilations point towards Saleem's split personality. His psychic split is emphasized by Saleem's continually speaking of himself in first and third person. This makes him an omniscient and limited first person narrator at the same time. Saleem appears to be a 'self-subverting' narrator, an aspect of narrative that suggests the post-modern concept of unstable identity. Multiplication of parentage places Saleem in a state of orphanhood and marginal status and thus he lacks a symbolic centre. In most of Rushdie novels, the main characters are set-off against strong alter egos. In *Midnight's Children*, Saleem Sinai's antagonist is Shiva. Shortly after their birth, the nurse Mary Pereira religiously had exchanged the two babies so that Saleem is in reality Shiva and Shiva is Saleem.

Saleem also has various names that stand for different roles he has to act out. 'I, Saleem Sinai, later variously called Snotnose, Stainface, Baldy, Sniffer, Buddha and even piece-of-the Moon' (9). 'Snotnose' stands for Saleem's telepathic abilities, 'Sniffer' stands for his degradation to the sub-human soldier called 'man-dog,' in the Sundarbans episode. Mutability of identity is reflected in Saleem's different names and various roles he plays in life and Mary Pereira, the nurse sings, 'Anything you want to be, you kin be/ you kin be just what-all you want' (383).

In *Midnight's Children* the reader is presented with an alternative view of human characters. In Saleem's words, 'To understand just one life, you have to swallow the world' (109). Everything leaks into everything else. Many more things have to be described. This is opposed to the idea of the unified character which can be mimed infinitely. In post-modern situation, one has a different principle for selecting details. In Rushdie's fiction, characters are at the mercy of Saleem's judgment. Saleem is the central consciousness and all other characters move round the central psychic state. Saleem selects, re-arranges. The perforated sheet syndrome informs the mind and consciousness of the characters. The perforated sheet metaphor stands for fragmented identity. Rushdie, like Brecht intentionally breaks the hold of mimetic forms, well-structured plot and life-like characters who make free choices and demand sympathy from the readers. In place of sympathy there is in *Midnight's Children* a distancing through reporting and commentary, parody and allegory. Characters in a Rushdie novel are under our critical attention and there is a kind of distancing between the reader and the character in the novel.

Further, characters in a Rushdie novel move into two worlds, the real and the unreal. His characters mostly belong to the world of the fable and folk tale. Midnight's children do possess supernatural powers at their birth. Ramram Seth, a soothsayer remains an example of India's mystic powers. One of the sections of Book One of *Midnight's Children* entitled 'Many-headed Monsters' begins with Amina Sinai undertaking a journey to the soothsayer Ramram Seth to know his predictions about her coming son. Ramram predicts a terrible monster to be born to Amina. The prediction constitutes a riddle, an equivocation which surrounds the birth of Amina's son.

> A son Sahiba, who will never be older than his mother—neither older nor younger. There will be two heads—but you shall see only one—there will be knees and a nose, a nose and knees. Newspaper praises him, two mothers raise him! Bicyclists love him—but crowds will shove him! Sisters will weep; Cobra will creep... washing will hide him! Friends mutilate him—blood will betray him.... Spittons will brain him—doctors will drain him—Jungle will claim him—wizards reclaim him! Soldiers will try him—tyrants will fry him.... He will have sons without having sons! He will be old before he is old! And he will die...before he is dead (87-88).

Ramram's prediction comes true in the sense that Saleem with nose is actually Shiva with the knees. Saleem, as the story unfolds, appears to be the child of the departing Englishman Methwold and the low-caste woman Vanita and is subsequently exchanged at birth with Shiva who is the real son of Amina and Ahmed Sinai. But then Saleem is really hydra-headed, born of multiple parents, born as he is at midnight hour and hence never older than his country.

Monsters, fairies, witches, jinns, and other fantastic figures who haunt the popular imagination are found to inhabit the universe of the comic-epic prose tales of *Midnight's Children*. As Ahmed Sinai's assets are frozen by the Government his genitals are frozen and he is possessed by jinns in the bottle. In the *Arabian Nights* tales, jinns occasionally appeared in bottles to be released from captivity. In *Midnight's Children* characters are caricatures as is evidenced from Saleem's description of the metamorphosis of his father who turns into a red eyed monster.

> And so it was my doing that Ahmed Sinai fell, in those days after my birth, into the twin fantasies which were to be his undoing, into the unreal worlds of the jinns and of the land beneath the sea. At six O' clock every evening, Ahmed Sinai entered the world of the jinns and every morning, his eyes red, his head throbbing with the fatigue of his night-long battle, he came unshaven to the breakfast table, and with the passage of the years, the good mood of the time before he shaved was replaced by the irritable exhaustion of his war with the bottled spirits. If Ahmed Sinai is transformed into a monster, Saleem's real father, Methwold undergoes a remarkable metamorphosis. From a Samson like figure, he changes into what Padma calls 'a baldie' (114).

His change is related to the transformation of the British Empire into yet another European country. In *Midnight's Children*, male characters are mostly inactive and impotent and serve as caricatures. Saleem, Ahmed Sinai, Aadam and Nadir Khan are sometimes given to dream and hallucination and are found to be unreal. Again these characters have real life connotations. Rushdie believes that the fantastic and unreal are far more reliable modes of storytelling and are often a more accurate mirror of truth. In *Midnight's Children*, the magical and fantastic has a significant place. Uncle Hanif is successful as a film maker when he adopts the fantastic and unrealistic mode of storytelling in his film, 'The Lovers of Kashmir.' His realistic attempt to tell stories falls flat because it is in the magical and fantastic that our deepest desires are captured. Similarly Saleem avoids Padma's demand for realistic 'what nextism' for a bizarre mode of storytelling pertaining to a country (India) where reality is stranger than fiction. Midnight's children like the newborn nation are in possession of magical qualities. The magical and fantastic symbolizes the new hope and powers of regeneration that are granted by the almighty to the children born at the midnight hour, August 15, 1947. Female characters too born at that precise hour do possess magical charm.

Midnight's Children contains a fascinating portrait of the life and character of female characters. In fact, the women are the target group of readers whom the novel addresses. Saleem addresses his tales to Padma, the female narratee who sometimes interferes, comments and criticizes. She is Saleem's servant, mistress and plays a significant role in the novel. The word 'Padma' means lotus and is the symbol of one who was born in slime and mud. She is illiterate and is after sensation and what happened nextism. Saleem disapproves Padma's aesthetic counsels. He thinks that he is superior to her in intellect. In spite of the author's patriarchal bias, rather unconscious, against female intellect, Padma remains a true critic of Saleem. Her masterful control over Saleem can be felt when we see that she is Saleem's typical audience. Her critical response to the storytelling is superb. She dislikes any breaking of the narrative spell.

> I must intercept myself. I wasn't going today because Padma has started getting irritated whenever my narration becomes self-conscious, whenever, like an incompetent puppeteer, I reveal the hands holding the strings (72).

Padma has all the qualities of a good housewife in a typical Hindu household. But there are women in the novel who are masculine and threatening just as men are weak and impotent. Naseem, the beautiful daughter is seen by the young doctor Dr Aziz through a perforated sheet held high by threatening masculine women. After marriage, Naseem transforms into an imposing figure and develops a threatening skill to invade her daughter's and husband's dreams. She is justly called reverend mother. The metamorphosis of mothers into monsters refers to the typical cult of mother construction in the Indian psyche. Naseem's absolute control over kitchen and her refusal to serve food brings Dr Aziz to the point of death. This is an example of mother's nurturing and destructive qualities. Indira Gandhi who, in this novel, has been repeatedly called 'widow,' is the mother of Emergency. The appellation widow signifies the drying up of emotions, harshness etc. It also means uncontrolled power over the household or the country. Mother cult is associated with the nature (*prakriti*) *vis-à-vis* male principle (*purusha*) as enunciated by Sankhya System of Indian Philosophy.

> We the magical children of midnight, were hated, feared destroyed by the widow who was not only prime minister of India but also aspired to be Devi, the Mother Goddess in her most terrible aspect, possessor of the Shakti of the Gods, a multi-limbed divinity, with a centre parting and schizophrenic hair (522).

However, the exaggeration makes Indira Gandhi a ridiculous character and some critics find in the portrayal of the character of the widow an indecent hasty authorial taste. But then the widow in the novel remains a part of the history, rather than a symbol of the post-colonial agency of the dark period of the emergency and the curtailment of democratic rights. Post-colonial subject is fragmented, has multiple identities as opposed to the static and fixed concept of characterization. In *Midnight's Children* the reader is presented with an alternative view of human character as the sum total of social circumstances. A post-colonial character is born handcuffed to history. Since the publication of Salman Rushdie's *Midnight's Children*, characters in post-colonial Indian English fiction have been found to be grappling with the concept of nation, race, history and community. In other words, with Rushdie, Indian English fiction got rid of its fear of life. In an interview, Anita Desai observed that '*Midnight's Children* gave her the courage and artistic room to move into the public sphere in her own fiction.'[1] Rushdie's art of playfulness made room for 'discursive space for her where there was none before' (Josna E. 201).

NOTE

1. Anita Desai, Personal Interview, S. Hadley, Massachusetts, November 1972.

5

Major Characters

SALEEM SINAI

Saleem Sinai happens to be the principal narrator in *Midnight's Children*. He is the central consciousness in the novel and, is empowered at birth with magical powers.

Saleem is one of 1001 children who are born at the midnight hour of August 15, 1947. Midnight's children are imagined to be born with magical power and supernatural skill. This is because a new nation full of hope and immense possibilities comes into existence. But subsequently, as the new nation starts its journey, many of the children will surely perish, and thus hope in the ideal of progress and democratic institutions will disappear. Events in the private spheres of the children of the midnight and in the public sphere coincide. Birth of Saleem and the birth of new Indian nation accidentally take place at the same time. The co-incidence of two births (birth of the hero and that of the country) constitutes the basic premise and the rest of the story follows as a sequence. But then Saleem is not Prince Hamlet and is not born to do great things.

The hero, Saleem Sinai has a Muslim name but he is fathered by a Christian and mothered by a Hindu woman and as a result, is an Indian by religion and nationality. He is brought up by Muslim parents whom he thinks his original parents. He makes efforts to move from the margin to the central position. He tries to create his identity by an act of writing. He is destined to be an eccentric and his narrative occasionally drifts into dream and nightmare. The reader is shuffled between the future, present and the past in an unchronological manner. The unities of time and place are not stable. As the narrator tends to see himself in both the first and third person, the reality of the characters as separate entities gets blurred. Saleem is depicted as enslaved by environment, the perennial victim of the accident of his birth and is doomed to bear the burden of history. The interplay of the personal and national histories tries to give a unity of sorts to the novel and shapes the personality of the narrator. Saleem, in post-colonial India, is born a marginal man, an average peripheral man having no say in the course of things that take place around him. In another sense, he stands as a symbol of universal little man who became, becomes and will always become the victim of great events like war, violence, riot and the partition of the motherland at the sweet will of the politicians. At one point, Saleem raises a pertinent question about his position in the scheme of things, 'Who, what am I? My answer! I am the sum total of everything that went before me, of all I have seen been done, of everything done to me' (457). Then again, 'Why, owing to accidents of birth prophecy etcetera, must I be responsible for language riots and after Nehru who,—why alone of all the five hundred million, should I have to bear the burden of history?' (457).

It is a Hamletian dilemma. Saleem raises a fundamental question, the universal mystery of unmerited suffering. 'Why me?'—he asks like Job in *The Old Testament*. His life is shown as ruled by history which is his destiny and there is limited choice for average little man.

'No choice?—None, when was there over?' (503). Saleem discovers that he assumes many identities and not a fixed one. Most significant of them all, he identifies himself with a landlord in UP ordering his peasants to set his surplus grain on fire and starve to death. He, on another occasion, becomes the consciousness of the so-called free India and experiences the life and agony of the multitudes of Indians. At this point, Saleem, the narrator, becomes the author's fictional alter ego, who sustains many identities and captures within his person the expectations of the common people; tensions and paradoxes of independence. Through the device of interlocking the destinies of man and the nation, Saleem like his creator becomes a historical witness to the emergence of a new post-colonial and modern era in the history of the country. Saleem's presentation of history has been compared to the pickling process which preserve eatables and makes them tastier than in their original state. As Saleem, the narrator observes, 'To pickle is to give immortality' (549). Posterity interested in the Indian history of the post-colonial times can whet their appetites by reading the spicy and chutneyfied version of Indian history in *Midnight's Children*. Saleem remains a great storyteller and Padma is the hypothetical Shaharyar type listener. Who does not know that women are eternal lovers of gossip and tales? Saleem represents the type of Indian storytellers of *Panchatantra*, *Vetal Pancha Vinsati*. There is no end to storytelling either in India or in Arabia.

As the story unfolds, we find that Saleem crashes into history on a runaway bicycle. In other words, he meets with an accident when he hurtles down the slope of a road to crash into the head of the first of the processions urging a linguistic division of the Bombay state. As a result of the jolt he becomes suddenly aware of the thousand other children born in India during the first hour of independence. He, in an amusing way, remains in telepathic contact with the surviving 581 out of them. During Emergency, a dark period in democratic India, 420 including Saleem are imprisoned together. By another stroke of fate, Saleem finds himself in Pakistan and participates in the historic coup that imposes Martial Law in Pakistan under the dictatorship of Ayub Khan. Later, at a subsequent time, Saleem joins the liberation war in Bangladesh. Thus the history of not one but three nations is closely linked with the fate of Saleem and other children of the midnight. Also, there are frequent summaries of previous events to refresh the reader's memory. Some such real events in India's post-colonial history, like partition riots, the war with China and Pakistan, sterilization programme during Emergency, corruption in public life and the like are realistically represented. The presentation of a realistic framework in the novel makes some critics depict Saleem as a character in the realist mode and for the misery of whom we are supposed to have tragic emotion. But the fact is that Saleem himself is allegorized in such a way that he becomes one of the devices in the communication of the story. He is multiplied like other characters and is one among the one thousand and one midnight's children whose stories could not be given for lack of space. The reader can imagine a close connection between Saleem and Ganesh, the mythical storyteller of the *Mahabharata*. As a storyteller, Saleem has Ganesh like skill. Ganesh of the *Mahabharata* is the patron-deity of art and literature. Rushdie states in an interview,

> The legend of Ganesh is the legend of disputed parentage.... Now it seemed to me that since Saleem's entire ancestry is also very murky and disputed, it was correct to give him, as a mythological ancestor, somebody with disputed ancestry with a disputed family line (Kunapipi 91).

Consequently, the identity of Saleem, the principal character in *Midnight's Children* has been problematised. He appears to be a bundle of contradictory feelings and emotions. He is playful but remains serious. He moves in the world of fancy and imagination but does not seem to be an unreal character in the fiction. He bears a title Sinai which has a Biblical connotation. Saleem draws upon myth and also on popular culture like folklore, cinema. This is done to enforce destabilization of "history's fixity." He casts himself as omniscient and omnipotent a narrator in the fashion of mythical Vishnu or Brahma—'The all knowing, all seeing and all wise'[1] but at the same time, he playfully identifies himself with the elephant headed Ganesh—because of his nose. Ceative act of writing becomes the paradigmatic act for Saleem as creation becomes the Karmic act for Vishnu. There is an assertion of the writer as all-powerful.

In Saleem's post-colonial India, things have gradually started falling apart. The cracking up of his body that he refers to is a similar act. Saleem represents the post-colonial India, politically and geographically too. In his tale he describes himself as a 'swallower of lives' and comments, 'to know me, just the one of me, you'll have to swallow the toe as well. Consumed multitudes are jostling and shoving inside me' (9). These multitudes cause him to crack up. The disintegration of Saleem's body accelerates as the story progresses until the last section when he describes his 'death.' The cracks are described literally and as yet metaphorically. There is a fictional relationship between the body of the individual and the body politic of the nation.

> My poor body, singular, unlovely, buffeted by too much history...has started coming apart at the seams. In short, I am literally disintegrating, slowly for the moment, although there are signs of acceleration. I ask you only to accept that I shall eventually crumble into (approximately) six hundred and thirty million particles of anonymous, and necessarily oblivious dust (37).

The Emergency was declared in India in 1975 when Indira Gandhi suspended civil liberties and introduced autocratic dictatorship. This event, an event of betrayal is portrayed in Saleem's narrative as a 'six hundred and thirty-five day long midnight' (443). On the political level this dark event translates as a violent confrontation between the two rival children of midnight, Shiva and Saleem, between 'knees and a nose' (478). In April 1976, under the pretext of civic beautification and slum clearance, Saleem finds 'the joints of my nemesis thundering towards me' (430). He is imprisoned and undergoes forced sterilization in Benares.

Saleem's narrative draws to a close around August 15, 1978 when his hypersensitive nose inhales mixed smells—on the one hand, 'the excitement of coming Independence Day,' and on the other 'most tarnished perfumes, disillusion, venality, cynicism' (457). The myth of freedom appears no longer what it was. Perhaps, it was a dream insufficiently imagined. 'New myths are needed; but that's none of my business' (458).

The hero of *Midnight's Children* has, at the moment of birth, an uncertain parentage. The narrative throws into disbelief the authenticity of his blood-link between himself and the rich businessman Ahmed Sinai and Amina Sinai who, he claims, are his biological parents. Due to an act of cradle switching, the baby Saleem born to a poor woman Vanita, gets a life of privilege and comfort. Actually, he is the son of a poor Hindu woman Vanita, wife of a musician Wee Willie by an Englishman William Methwold. Thus at birth, he remains the confluence of world religions and represents the post-colonial India which is multi-religious and multi-cultural—as opposed to the concept of purity of race or religion. His face represents the map of India. This child of midnight has four possible fathers (Ahmed Sinai, Nadir Khan, Wee Willie Winkie and Methwold) and three mothers (Vanita, Amina Sinai and Mary Parveira). As a narrator, he takes upon himself the responsibility of reporting rather re-writing the history of the new nation which is of his own age and he is in a hurry. He must finish the tale, (so many stories are to be told; he tells Padma, his female audience) before his body disintegrates. And his is only the one version of the story; there are many points of view and many versions.

The narrator speaks in first and third person and hence his narration is subject to the judgment and criticism of the readers. Saleem thus poses as an unreliable narrator and his art of narration is shaped by the female narratee Padma who shapes, controls and commands the narrative. In *Midnight's Children*, Saleem appears to bc thc author's alter ego. Rushdie re-creates history by making his hero, rather anti-hero participate in the process of history shaping itself. On the very opening page of the novel, Saleem Sinai announces that he was born 'mysteriously handcuffed to history' and later, he became 'heavily embroiled in Fate.' As the story proceeds we realize that it is not only the fate of an individual but also that of the entire nation. A new nation is born, though metaphorically, at the midnight hour and subsequently it is found that there is not one nation but three. Birth of Saleem coincides with the famous 'tryst with destiny' speech of the first Prime Minister of Independent India, who made the speech in the Central Hall of the Parliament at midnight on 15 August in 1947. The hero of *Midnight's Children* and a new nation are born at exactly the same time and hence the fate of the two are linked together. This part of the narration bears the mark of an excellent item of authorial fantasy. Individual remains the victim and at the same time, maker, of history. Saleem anticipates the author himself in the sense that Rushdie was born in June 1947 and two months later, the British left India.

PADMA—THE FEMALE NARRATEE

Character of Padma in *Midnight's Children* evokes much interest and criticism among the readers and the critics alike. Along with Saleem, the narrator, she remains the principal female character who contributes towards the shaping of the entire narrative. In other words, she remains the co-creator of the narrative. She is the female audience to whom the entire narrative is addressed. She has been very loyal, 'faithful and a great devotee to Saleem and loves him from the core of her heart.' Critics have noticed in her and in her relationship with Saleem, a reflection of traditional Hindu wife who is self-sacrificing and fully devoted to her husband. Saleem is in fact a fertile storyteller but he is emasculated while Padma is illiterate and seems to be driven by intense physical urges. She is portrayed as Saleem's female narratee eager for sensation, what happened nextism and linear narrative. The tension between Padma's 'what happened nextism' (39) and Saleem's need to conceal, shapes the entire narrative. In other words, their union leads to the creation of the fictional universe. The Samkhya philosophy views the whole universe as the creation of two complementary agents: *Purusha* and *Prakriti*. The former stands for masculinity and the latter, femininity. Padma may be termed as the eternal feminine principle and acts the role of a devoted wife in the contour of the text. She also plays a much bigger role of good wife, secretary and friend to Saleem as the Indian poet Kalidasa imagined. The narrative of *Midnight's Children*' gradually subverts this hypothesis that together Saleem and Padma is a very traditional couple. As the story unfolds, it appears that they are simply partners. Padma is Saleem's potential female narrateee. She is the hypothetical Shaharyar type listener of tales and who does not know that women are eternal lovers of gossip and tales? Notwithstanding her paramount role in the creation of the novel, Padma has been subjected to gender injustice. The narrator Saleem while recognizes the indispensable role of Padma in the creation of the tale, does not fail to betray his patriarchal bias.

'And certainly Padma is leaking into me. As history pours out of my fissured body, my lotus is quietly dripping in, with her down-to-earthery, and her paradoxical superstition, her contradictory love of the fabulous' (38). Saleem's contention that Padma is after sensation and is driven by physical urges has been contested by feminist reading of the text. In a note of contradiction Saleem states that Padma is not only the female narratee, but also his 'necessary ear' (149). She interrupts, comments and criticizes. She is indispensable for the framing of the narrative.

'How to dispense with Padma? How to give up her ignorance and superstition, necessary counterweights to my miracle-laden omniscience.... Our Padma is gone and I miss her' (150).

A feminist interpretation of the portrayal of the character of Padma might be profitable as it may help us to evaluate her role in the making of the narrative. Critics[2] have observed that the sexist bias operates against nearly all women characters in the novel. Padma, it appears, has been a prey of male chauvinism in the novel. She is depicted through her animal instincts. Saleem mentions her as 'Padma—our plump Padma...sulking magnificently (she can't read. Padma strong, jolly, a consolation for my last days. But definitely a bitch in the manager)' (24). This is followed by a still more damaging hint. "Padma snorts, wrist smacks against forehead. 'Okay, starve, starve, who cares two pice?' Another louder, conclusive snort.... Thick of waist, somewhat fairy of forearm, she flounces, gesticulates, exists. Poor Padma" (24). This is a very damaging portrait of the central female character who is compared to a bitch and who snorts, moves her hand up down up and so on. She is portrayed as illiterate, ignorant as well. Saleem again says that Paddma 'really—truly was a witch' (381). This only indicates his male attitude towards his female partner but for whose active co-operation he would remain impotent and impotent he is though metaphorically.

At the beginning, the reader is presented with the picture of a happy conjugal relationship between the spouses who have, it appears, lived together for a long time. Padma appears to be a traditional Hindu wife who remains dedicated to the well-being and comfort of her husband. She cooks food for Saleem, prepares his bed and remains busy for him. But her role has no appreciation. She is simply ignored and she becomes disappointed. Nonetheless, she remains submissive, honest and devoted. Saleem writes and writing is considered a masculine act and hence, he monopolizes time, history and politics. Act of cooking or making bed or other domestic chores are considered the act of the females and are of secondary importance. Padma's works only present her as a mere stereotype. The reader is presented with binaries between order and chaos; intellect and emotion; literate and illiterate and the like. Saleem derides her for illiteracy; she is the feminine 'other' or 'lack' or 'absence'. The social order founded by male powers in post-colonial society in particular, generates gender prejudices. One's role in the society determines one's gender. Cooking food, washing clothes, giving birth to children, making beds for husbands are considered women's trades and the rest are superior works and are for men. So man has power over women. Saleem takes Padma's loyalty for granted. He thinks it his male prerogative to avoid or deceive Padma. He does not fulfil Padma's carnal craving as he puts it, or her physical demand. Nonetheless he claims that Padma is a sensual raven. After passing a long period of togetherness, Saleem avows that he is no good in bed, Padma has been deceived into believing that Saleem must be physically fit. Saleem, very like many Indian husbands who prefer parading their masculine power at home, fails to understand that her requirements are emotional and psychic. She requires a loving, caring and sympathetic life-partner. Saleem is eccentric and has no time for this rustic girl. It is her love for Saleem that has trapped her. She pines for his love. 'So then I thought, how to go back to this man who will not love me and only does some foolish writer? (Forgive, Saleem baba, but I must tell it truly. And love, to us women, is the greatest thing of all)' (193). But, alas, if Saleem could give her a caring and sympathetic touch. Padma is a Hindu woman and she genuinely loves a man who is an impotent Muslim widower. This speaks volumes for her devotional love. Her pitiable plight is revealed in the following statement made by Saleem:

> Our Padma bibi, long suffering, tolerant consoling, is beginning to behave exactly like a traditional Indian wife. (And I, with my distances and self-absorption, like a husband?) Of late, in spite of my stoic fatalism about the spreading cracks, I have smelled, on Padma's breath, the dream of an alternative (but impossible) future; ignoring the implacable finalities of inner fissures, she has begun to exude the bittersweet fragrance of hop-for-marriage. My dung-lotus, who remained impervious for so long to the sneer lipped barbs hurled by our workforce of downy-forearmed women; who placed her co-habitation with me outside and above all codes of social propriety, has seemingly succumbed to a desire for legitimacy...in short, although she has not said a word on the subject, she is waiting for me to make an honest woman of her. The perfume of her sad hopefulness permeates her most innocently solicitous remarks (384-85).

It appears Padma has sold her life for Saleem's love. Saleem can't write in her absence. But he takes her presence to be granted. As he is a male, he does not reciprocate his urge. He degrades and exploits her but expects her to be loyal. She exclaims "This love, mister, Padma is wailing, 'It will drive a woman to craziness'" (193).

In this novel the character of Padma is portrayed more in absence than in presence. Her absence describes her family background and past. She is discarded as she is considered a bundle of emotion but the readers have sympathy for her. Saleem goes three generations back to begin his story and compels the readers to know a lot of lives besides his own life. Padma's story, her past and present, her parents—are lost, excluded. Padma is better portrayed in absence. She is the 'lack,' the 'other.'

Padma is depicted as the 'lotus Goddess' in the novel. She had been named after the lotus Goddess by her mother, whose most common appellation amongst village folk is 'The One who possesses Dung' (24). *Padma* the lotus grew out of Vishnu's navel and from which Brahma himself was born, Padma the source, the mother of time (194-95). She is adored as a deity. The fictional Padma offers a subversion of context. She remains Saleem's disdained other and is presented as a female who cares for only sensationalism. She is only a prey of illiteracy. The novelist presents this paradigm for the female characters in general. Padma is mentioned as a 'submissive soul' or 'agonised self' who works according to her master's desire. She is not a free soul in a male dominated situation. Kate Millet considers it the 'power-nexus' (6). The situation of woman is that—she, a free and autonomous being like all creatures—nevertheless finds herself living in a world where men compel her to assume the status of the other.[3] Padma in *Midnight's Children* is depicted as a devoted nurse who does nursing work when Saleem is in fever. Such feminine and graceful acts of kindness and love are ample proof that she is a partner not only for bed but for life. But she is a prey of male ego and masculine might and her role in Saleem house is degraded. Women's work has long been downgraded and devalued when compared to man's work, male muscular strength has been prized above the female capacity for physical endurance, men have been the owners of wealth and property, the wielders of authority, the holders of power, the achievers, the doers, the go getters, while women have been barred from such apparently desirable positions or behaviours[4] (McLeod 18).

A Marxist reading of *Midnight's Children* emphasizes Padma's symbolical value as a plebeian commentator. This interpretation focuses on the 'hegemonic prevalence of the central/bourgeois/male agents over the plebeian/female identity' (Picincco 244). Marxist critics maintain that a complete national identification may be searched for in the combination of Saleem and Padma. The text deliberately focuses attention on Saleem's story but Padma's plebeian lineage is totally abrogated. It is for the feminist reading to unearth the missing narrative.

The gap between Saleem's elitist education and Padma's imagined illiteracy is a sad reflection on social reality. Padma has been sketched out as a stereotype, as a character representative of her gender. Critics have debated over the issue whether Padma is a listener or reader of Saleem's writing. Notwithstanding the fact that Saleem's narration is not necessarily directed at her only, Padma paradoxically covers the function of both a listener and reader. Politically speaking, Padma represents the gullible people of the subcontinent who are easily duped by the demagogues in the post-colonial country. But then Padma is not a passive receptor of 'disembodied voice of the national conscience but a literary critic' (Brennan 101). Her passivity as a traditional Indian wife turns out to be extremely productive to the text. Her identity or function in the novel may be defined with reference to her relationship to Saleem, the narrator and not Saleem, the person. The *Midnight's Children* is the final result of the union between the two in a special sense. It is this union on a higher level which leads to the fertile combination. A. Banerjee points out, 'together they make history' (Banerjee 25). According to one opinion, it is the woman who prevails in the end. Padma's victory is not associated with personal victory. She has made and unmade Saleem, the creator of the fictional universe. Saleem could not do without Padma. At one point he announces 'Women have made me and also unmade.' Notwithstanding the passive role assigned to her in the novel, Padma remains an active co-ordinator in the framing of the grand tale which is *Midnight's Children*.

MAJOR SHIVA

Towards the end of the novel *Midnight's Children*, Saleem's body disintegrates and Shiva, his alter-ego, takes over. Shiva embodies the force of disintegration and chaos. Shiva is the genetic son of Ahmed and Amina Sinai, who has been raised in extreme poverty. As a fictional character, Shiva in his violent action, bears close resemblance to the Puranic God of destruction who is the husband of Parvati. Saleem's body starts developing cracks and fissures when the nascent post-colonial Indian state deviates from Nehruvian model of secular democracy at the moment when Indira Gandhi declares Emergency which means curtailment of the democratic rights of the citizens. Saleem falls into pieces metaphorically as the Nehruvian dream of a secular India dreamt by the children of midnight shatters into pieces and the divisive forces of religion, caste, and language become uppermost. As the fictional character Saleem disintegrates, Shiva is in control of the narrative; he becomes Indira Gandhi's henchman. Politically Indira Gandhi (fictional character 'the widow') takes over, the moment Nehruvian ideal of secular democracy begins to crumble in post-colonial India. By a cinematic act of the exchange of babies at birth Saleem is given a life of privilege and comfort while Shiva is doomed to a life of poverty and misery. Shiva represents the dispossessed multitudes for whom ideology, order and meaning have no value. Saleem's concern with order and meaning constitutes a mere emblem of class privilege. Shiva represents the proletariat class and he stands for unreason, unmeaning, chaos and violence. But then violence does not serve any meaningful purpose. If Shiva does not possess any constructive political ideology or vision, this is because of a vacuum in the socio-political thinking of our neo-colonial masters. All babies are equal at birth and there is no just explanation why one person is born to wealth and another, doomed to poverty and misery. Shiva represents the majority of India's children who are born to a state of abject poverty and misery and swell the rank of the dispossessed and the disgruntled. In most cases, they embrace an ideology of violence and chaos. It is for the reader to make a choice between either Saleem or Shiva as the true mirror of post-colonial India. Antagonism between Saleem and Shiva remains a crucial political issue which plagues the history and politics of the post-colonial country even today.

> I was obliged to come to the conclusion that Shiva, my rival, my changeling brother, could no longer be admitted into the forum of my mind, for reasons which were, I admit ignoble. I was afraid he would discover what I was sure I could not conceal from him—the secrets of our birth. Shiva, for whom the world was things, for whom history could only be explained as the continuing struggle of oneself against the crowd,

> would certainly insist on claiming his birthright; and, aghast at the very notion of my knock-kneed antagonist replacing me in the blue room of my childhood.... I resolved that my destructive, violent alter ego should never again enter the increasingly fractious councils of the Midnight's Children's Conference; that I would guard my secret—which had once been Mary's—with my very life (339).

As a child of midnight, Shiva is given the gift of the war. He is Saleem's adversary and does not care for idealism. He rejects Saleem's search for meaning and purpose because poverty leaves no room for philosophizing. He is condemned to a life of criminality. He espouses his philosophy in categorical terms, 'there is no third principle, there is only money and poverty and have and lack...and the world is no place for dreamers...look at Birla and Tata and all the powerful they make things' (255). In the course of things, Saleem withdraws into his own private shell and Shiva rises. Spirituality is called a bluff and criminality asserts itself. Shiva, as years roll on, the amoral child of Midnight asserts his power. He stands as an enemy to Saleem's narrative power, Saleem's concern for order, history and nation. Shiva 'is the true generator of human affairs, as it is Shiva who is the only one of the midnight's children to father another generation' (Kortenaar 44). He incidentally creates a new race of children, bastard products of his illegitimate relations with numerous society ladies. Shiva may have an imagined reflection on some real-life politicians-cum-criminals who rule the roost particularly in the northern part of post-colonial India. Shiva is no dreamer of high things like sacrifice, sympathy for fellow beings; so are the most of India's politicians, by fate, midnight's politicians of this great land. The mythic dimension is implied and is kept in the background. The readers can make their own connection by association.

Let us have a look at the career of Major Shiva. The story is pieced together from Parvati's accounts. Shiva found himself elevated in social status as well as military rank, and was invited to a thousand and one different gatherings—banquets, musical soirees, bridge parties, diplomatic receptions, party political conferences, great fairs and smaller, local fetes, school sport days and fashionable balls—to be applauded by the noblest and fairest in the land. The legends of his exploits (particularly sexual exploits) made the people touch him through the magical film of his myth. They could not speak to him as they would to an ordinary human being. The Indian army which was at that time fighting a political battle against proposed expenditure cuts, understood the value of so charismatic an ambassador, and permitted the hero to circulate amongst his influential admirers; Shiva espoused his new life with a will. He grew a luxuriant moustache and engaged in political chitchat and declared himself a firm admirer of Mrs Gandhi, largely because of his hatred for her opponent Morarji Desai, who was intolerably ancient, drank his own urine and, as Chief Minister of Bombay, had once been responsible for the banning of alcohol, and the persecution of young goondas. Shiva's thoughts were entirely taken up with ladies. He was becoming a 'notorious seducer; a ladies'-man; a cuckolder of the rich; in short, a stud' (487).

Saleem becomes able to claim one of Shiva's offsprings as his own son. His wife Parvati—the witch whom he later married after his return to the magicians' ghetto called to Shiva and Shiva came. The thing that drew him into the ghetto was quite simply the magic of Parvati-the-witch. Saleem was not in the ghetto when Major Shiva arrived by motorcycle.

> There are ironies here, which must not pass unnoticed; for had not Shiva risen as Saleem fell? Who was the slum-dweller now, and who looked down from commanding heights? Major Shiva came to the magicians' ghetto and strode through the cruel streets of the slum with a strange expression on his face, which combined the infinite disdain for poverty (486).

From the beginning there were knees and a nose, a nose and knees. Shiva is known for his knees. His glittering life became for him a daily humiliation. He could re-interpret the advances of the beautiful ladies. By placing their love-notes beneath their toes they were obliging him to kneel demeaningly at their feet.

He felt an old violence being renewed in him, a hatred for these high-ups and their power. When the Emergency offered Shiva-of-the-knees the chance of grabbing some power for himself, he did not wait to be asked a second time. Shiva, destroyer of the midnight's children, had also fulfilled the other role lurking in his name, the function of Shiva-lingam, of Shiva-the-procreator, so that a new generation of children, begotten by midnight's darkest child, was being raised towards the future.

The character of Shiva shows a deviation from the Shiva myth 'Shiva the God of destruction, who is also most potent of deities, Shiva, greatest of dancers; who rides on a bull; whom no force can resist' (264). The fictional character Shiva is fallible. He uses offensive words and is a criminal. He expresses no regret for his action. He joins the election fraud. In Benares, Shiva's town, Saleem is sterilized under the orders of Major Shiva, his arch rival. Shiva in the end gets himself voluntarily vasectomised. That may seem to be the end of the race of midnight's children. But it remains an item of irony that Aadam Sinai, Shiva's natural son begotten by him through Parvati before her marriage with Saleem (who has been made impotent) 'was growing up carrying onwards the characteristics of *Midnight's Children* of whom Saleem and not Shiva was the true representative' (Mathur 234).

But then the alternative to Saleem should not be the figure of irrational destructiveness. The portrayal of the character of Shiva drives home the fact that if we reject the idea of the secular nation and its history, we will definitely land in chaos and anarchy. Shiva therefore 'represents the dispossessed without a stake in the nation, the political threat to Saleem's India' (Kortenaar 44). He is made to represent chaos and unmeaning. His narration is 'without conscious thought'. Saleem instinctively feels responsible for his own fate and is always haunted by a feeling of guilt for taking the place of Shiva. Often he blames the nurse Mary Pareira for his destiny as she is responsible for Shiva's twist of fate. Fate and history conspire against both Saleem and his alter ego, Shiva from the very first moment of their existence. This incident of the exchange of babies makes the readers aware of a simple fact that no one can choose the place, circumstances and historical situation in which we are born. Like Saleem, his rival, Shiva is the victim of fate and history. And again Shiva reacts in his own way and creates his part of history—victim as well as protagonist.

DR AADAM AZIZ

In Forster's *A Passage to India* Dr Aziz, a fictional character, has been portrayed as a Muslim doctor. Forster's Aziz is a Muslim, a marginal character and not a full-blooded Indian. Aziz is portrayed on the basis of the author's racial prejudices. To his white authorial imagination, Aziz appears as a Muslim stereotype and not an Indian national though the national freedom struggle was at its peak when the book was written and published in 1924. This missing narrative in Forster's text has been supplemented by Rushdie in his famous novel *Midnight's Children* (1981) by depicting Dr Aziz as a German-educated Indian national. 'The first national subject textualized in Rushdie is the German-educated doctor Aadam Aziz' (Nalini Natarajan 170). He happens to be Saleem's imagined grandfather and the narrator grandson describes the past events that had taken place in the life of the grandfather since 1915 in a tone of playfulness, comedy and satire. Aadam Aziz returns home with a void in his head—European skepticism has destroyed his faith in religion and rituals. This is described in a very funny way. The passage is a remarkable document of the state of mind of a Europe-returned Indian in the first part of twentieth century.

> One Kashmiri morning in the early spring of 1915, my grandfather Aadam Aziz hit his nose against a frost-hardened tussock of earth while attempting to pray. Three drops of blood plopped out of his left nostril, hardened instantly in the brittle air and lay before his eyes on the prayer mat, transformed into rubies. Lurching back until he knelt with his head once more upright, he found that the tears which had sprung to his eyes had solidified, too, and at that moment, as he brushed diamonds contemptuously from his lashes, he resolved never again to kiss earth for any God or man. This decision, however, made a hole in him, a vacancy

> in a vital inner chamber, leaving him vulnerable to woman and history. Unaware of this at first, despite his recently concluded medical training, he stood up, rolled the prayer-mat, and holding it under his right arm surveyed the valley through clear, diamond free eyes (4).

Saleem, the grandson narrator takes pains to reveal the secret of his grandfather's altered vision. The grandfather or Aziz, as a young man, had spent five years, five springs away from home. Now returning, he saw through travelled eyes. He felt sad to be at home as if the old place had resented the return of this educated young man. The years in Germany had returned him to a hostile environment. He developed a void, a permanent hole in the inner chamber of his mind. However, Dr Aziz regained the re-integration of his self over the body of a woman patient, who later becomes his wife. She is the daughter of a rich landowner and is in *purdah* (veiled). The Doctor is allowed to see the patient through the holes in a sheet. As Aadam Aziz treats her patient in parts, he begins to imagine her as a whole. This synecdochic (from part to whole) imagination coincides with his imagining a whole Indian identity for himself instead of regional Kashmiri one. After marriage, Aziz told her wife to come out of *purdah* but Naseem Aziz finds the idea revolting. When the couple moves to Amritsar, Naseem finds herself exposed to the multiplicity of the country as Aziz sets fire to her *purdah* (veils).

'Buckets are brought, the fire goes out, and Naseem cowers on the bed as about thirty-five Sikhs, Hindus and untouchables throng in the smoke-filled room' (33). Aadam Aziz, after the purdah burning, calls his wife to shed his traditional inhibitions in favour of modernity. 'Forget about being a good Kashmiri girl. Start thinking about being a modern Indian woman' (33). We recall that Aziz's mother came out of purdah to finance her son's education.

The narrator gives an account of Aadam Aziz's personnel details and his claim for the position of a patriarch of a mythical dimension.

> I record that Dr Aziz was a tall man. Pressed flat against a wall of his family home, he measured twenty-five bricks or just six foot two. A strong man also. His beard was thick and red—and annoyed his mother, who said only Hajis should grow red beards. His hair was rather darker. His sky-eyes you know about. But the central feature of my grandfather's anatomy was neither color nor height, neither strength of arm nor straightness of back.... My grandfather's nose: nostrils fearing, curvaceous as dancers. Between them swells the nose's triumphal arch, first up and out, then down and under, sweeping into his upper lip. An easy nose to hit tussock with, I wish to place on record my gratitude to their organ—if not for it—who would have ever believed me to be truly my mother's son, my grandfather's grandson?—This colossal apparatus which was to be my birthright too. Doctor Aziz's nose—comparable only to the trunk of the elephant-headed God Ganesh—established incontrovertibly his right to be a patriarch (8).

That Saleem looks upon his natural grandfather (in a patriarchal society) as the source of his family-line is not without a purpose. He has a problem with his genealogy. Aadam, like the father of mankind in the Biblical story of Creation, 'sets history in motion' (12) the very moment when he was called on to treat the illness of Naseem Ghani, the daughter of a landowner in Kashmir. He is imagined to have two characteristics in common with his grandson—a large nose and a hole in the centre, 'leaving him vulnerable to women and history' (192). The comical description of the perforated sheet with a hole seven inches in diameter, through which Aadam Aziz was compelled to examine the diseased part of the body of his future wife is a strange feat of magic realism. This fun-provoking episode in the life of Aadam Aziz 'constitutes an improbable family heirloom and seems to underline the importance of fragments over the whole' (D'Souza 40).

NOTES

1. Syed Mujeebuddin, "*Midnight's Children* and its Indian Contexts" in *Rushdie's Midnight's Children—A Book of Readings* (ed.) Meenakshi Mukherjee, Pencraft International, Delhi, 2003, 149-164.
2. Charu Verma, "Padma's Tragedy: A Feminist Deconstruction of Rushdie's *Midnight's Children*" in *Feminism and Recent Fiction in English* (ed.) Sushila Singh, Prestige, New Delhi, 1991.
3. Helene Lamoure Eisenberg, "The Theme of Demission in the Works of Simone de Beauvoir" (Ph.D. Dissertation, University of California, Berkeley, 1978).
4. Sheila McLeod, "The Passion to be Masculine," *Lawrence's Men & Women* (1985 rpt. London, Paladin Grafton Books, 1987) 18.

6

Minor Characters

BOATMAN TAI

Boatman Tai has been portrayed as a puzzling character who speaks at times, in metaphors and riddles. He has no idea of his age, and makes his living as a simple ferryman. It is Tai who pointed out the significance of Aadam Aziz's nose, 'That's a nose to start a family on. There are dynasties waiting inside it' (8). Nobody could remember when Tai had been young. He had been seen plying the same boat across the Dal Lakes forever. He lived somewhere in the insanitary bowels of the old wooden-house quarter and his wife grew lotus roots and other vegetables on one of the many floating gardens. Tai himself used to admit cheerfully that he had no idea of his age. Neither did his wife, she said that he had already leathery skin when they married. His face was a sculpture of wind on water. He had two golden teeth and no other. In the town he had few friends.

The general opinion of Tai had been voiced long ago by Aadam Aziz's father, 'His brain fell out with his teeth' (9). It was an impression the boatman fostered by his chatter, which was fantastic and ceaseless. The sound carried over water and the lake people laughed at his monologues. People feared him because of his claim to an antiquity so immense, it defied numbering. Tai, metaphorically, stands for India's ancient past and wisdom of the ages. He made his simple living as a boatman, taking hay, goats, vegetables and wood across the lakes and people too. When he was running his taxi-service, he erected a pavilion in the centre of the shikara, a gay affair of curtains and canopy with cushions to match; and deodorized his boat with incense. The sight of Tai's shikara approaching, curtains flying, had always been for Dr Aziz, one of the defining images of the coming of spring. Soon the Sahibs would arrive and Tai would ferry them to the Shalimar Gardens and the King's Spring. He was the antithesis of change. He stands as a symbol of what is eternal about Indian wisdom, past glory, *vis-à-vis* the taboo. Young Aadam Aziz plunged into friendship with ageless Tai. He would ride in the shikara with Tai, squatting amongst goats, on a pile of straw. He loved Tai's stories. Tai was a great storyteller. He called Dr Aziz nakkoo, because of his long nose. Aziz became curious about Tai's age and asked, 'Tell, Taiji, how old, truly.' Tai pointed at the mountain and replied, 'So old, nakkoo; I have watched the mountains being born; I have seen emperors die.... I saw that Isa, that Christ, when he came to Kashmir. Smile, smile, it is your history I am keeping in my head' (11). He is as old as the Himalayas and sounds mystical. In one moment Tai appears not an ordinary human when he speaks in riddle. Aadam Aziz floated with Tai in his shikara again and again amid goats, hay, flowers, furniture and lotus roots. Tai would tell him, on the water, stories and more stories. It is from Tai, Dr Aziz heard about his noses. Tai tapped his left nostril and said, 'You know what this is, nakkoo? It's the place where the outside world meets the world inside you' (13).

But Tai remains the marginal character in the fictional universe. He is suspicious of the western science and modernity and, hence his clash with Aadam Aziz, a foreign-returned doctor and one of the central characters in the novel, is inevitable. He terms the medical profession an evil thing. This ageless boatman corresponds to Bakhtin's description of the grotesque body. Tai remains covered with excrement, does not take bath for years. This is a kind of defiance against what is normal, decent and civil. Tai has his double in Tai bibi, his wife, an equally grotesque and aged woman. She smells of excrement and subjects her customers to vicious abuse. Both of them use curses and obscene languages. Mr Tai's abuse and curses are directed at Dr Aziz, a foreign-returned medical man who is an evil intruder in the valley of paradise. Tai's invective is mostly directed at Dr Aziz's medical bag which contains modern instruments. This medical bag appears to be a symbol of western science and enlightenment and hence doctor's bag is Satanic. Tai's superstition against western science is phenomenal. He rails at the doctor's bag and calls it, 'a sister sleeping pigskin bag from abroad full of foreigners' tricks and concludes, 'that bag should fry in hell with the testicles of the ungodly' (20). In what is typical debunking of seriousness, Tai's language is non-serious and vulgar. He makes frequent use of images, words relating to genitals and acts of copulation. This is done in a way of degrading the value and respect shown to western science in the East. Boatman Tai exists in the realm of fantasy and hence there is a breach of chronology in his storytelling. Like the Puranic characters, he is ageless. In his poetic language, Rushdie describes the agelessness and something of the eternal and perennial in Tai. 'His face was a sculpture of wind on water' (14). An inversion of the things of the world is a marked feature of fantasy. It does not represent facts or what is real, instead invents facts and also, the real. The narrator observes, 'Reality can have metaphorical content; that does not make it less real' (200). Boatman Tai who is ageless, represents the accumulated wisdom of this ancient land which has witnessed the cycles of change through the ages.

MISS MARY PEREIRA

Miss Pereira does the job of a nurse at Dr Narlikar's nursing home. She, it appears, is devoted to her work in a special sense. She has a mission and is much inspired by one Marxist revolutionary Dr Bose. We find Dr Bose with Miss Pereira by his side—presides over the terminal stages of Vanita's twenty-four-hour labour. Vanita is a poor musician's wife and so the doctor and the nurse have a special eye on the birth of her child. At the approach of the midnight hour on August 15, 1947, Vanita had finally been relieved of a baby of remarkable size. There was another aching mother who also gave a midnight birth. She is Amina Sinai, wife of a rich businessman Ahmed Sinai. Poor man's wife Vanita died immediately after giving birth to her baby. Midwives had been instructed to wash and swaddle the newborn pair and now it is Miss Pereira who played her role, her act remains an act of supreme importance in the shaping of the narrative.

Miss Pereira, the nurse asked her mates to leave as she can do the work of washing the newborn babies single-handed. When she was alone—two babies in her hands—two lives in her power, she did her own private revolutionary act thinking that Joseph would certainly love her for this. For the moment she was impatient to do her contribution towards the proletarian revolution in her own way. She changed name-tags on the two huge infants, giving the poor boy a life of privilege and condemning the rich-born child to abject poverty. 'Love me Joseph!' was in Mary Pereira's mind and then the exchange of babies was done. Vanita's child was given to Amina Sinai. Thus Saleem Sinai became the chosen child of midnight, whose parents were not his parents and whose son would not be his own. The parents could not know about this criminal act of the exchange of babies. At three minutes past midnight, Vanita had haemorrhaged and died. Mary took the child of Amina's womb, wrapped it in green and brought it to Wee Willie Winkie, Vanita's husband, who did not know about this centre parting. This child was called Shiva.

Three days after the birth of the child, Mary Pereira had been consumed by remorse. She decided to make amends. She gave up her job at the nursing home and approached Amina Sinai who appointed her as an ayah. Thus Miss Mary Pereira devoted her life to bringing Saleem up and thus binding the rest of her days to the memory of her crime. She became one of Saleem's mothers and her eyes shone with motherhood. Thus she tried to expiate her sense of guilt.

NASEEM GHANI

The shy daughter of Ghani Sahib, Naseem Ghani appears before the inspecting eyes of her young doctor through the medium of a perforated sheet. She is the only daughter of the widower Ghani and remains in Veil. She complains of stomachache and Ghani Sahib calls in a Europe-returned doctor, Aziz. The doctor desires to see the patient first before he starts treatment and he does not find the patient, he is in confusion. Ghani's comments are amusing and ridiculous—

> You Europe-returned chappies forget certain things. Doctor Sahib, my daughter is a decent girl, it goes without saying. She does not flaunt her body under the noses of strange men. You will understand that you cannot be permitted to see her, no, not in any circumstances; accordingly I have required her to be positioned behind that sheet. She stands there like a good girl (19).

A perplexed Dr Aziz looked around that ill-lit bed chamber and saw that two lady wrestlers stood stiffily in the light each holding one corner of an enormous white bed sheet, their arms raised high above their heads so that the sheet hung between them like a curtain. The doctor made a wonderful discovery. In the very centre of the sheet, a hole had been cut, a crude circle about seven inches in diameter. The doctor and the invisible patient came into contact with that hole of seven inches diameter. It is an examination of the body of the young girl part by part and Naseem never repeated an illness. There was the matter of her stiff right knee which the doctor was obliged to manipulate through the hole in the sheet, and after a time the illness leapt upwards and so on. Gradually young Naseem Ghani passed into the realm of the dream in the mind of the inspecting doctor who came to have a picture of Naseem in his mind, a badly fitting collage of her severally-inspected parts. This phantasm of a partitioned woman began to haunt him. She moved into the front room of his mind. Magic of the perforated bed-sheet worked on both sides of the hole. In 1918 the Great War came to an end and at home Aziz's fall was complete. Doctor-patient relationship turned into that of lovers Ghani Sahib announced, 'Enough of this tamasha! No more need for this sheet tomfoolery! Drop it down, you women, these are young lovers now!' (28). In the month of March 1918, a gala marriage took place in the grounds of Ghani, the landowner's house. The dowry included among other valuables, the perforated sheet. Naseem, now, Dr. Aziz's wife landed up in Agra, the couple's new home.

On the second night, Aziz told his newly wed wife to move, to come out of her veils and be a modern Indian woman instead of remaining a decent Kashmiri girl. Naseem only started weeping into her pillow. She shrieked in horror. 'My God, what have I married? I know you Europe returned men. You find terrible women and then you try to make us girl be like them! Listen, Doctor Sahib, husband or no husband, I am not any bad word woman' (32). This was a battle Dr Aziz never won and it set the tone for their marriage. The family, as the years passed, turned into a place of devastating warfare. The young girl behind the sheet and the romantic doctor turned rapidly into stranger beings. Naseem, the beautiful daughter of Ghani had been seen through a perforated sheet held by muscular and threatening masculine women. But after marriage she soon is transformed from a shy young girl into a bloated, imposing figure. She becomes frequently threatening, masculine and bizarre just as Dr Aziz becomes weak and submissive. She experiences a fantastic transformation of her character when she develops 'fearsome ability to invade her daughter's and husband's dreams' (55). Transformation of Ghani's veiled daughter into a domineering mother in the Aziz household can be understood in the light of the portrayal of women characters in Rushdie novels. Repression is imagined to lead to resistance and sometimes, violence in the case of many Rushdie women. Naseem Ghani is rightly called Reverend Mother. The metamorphosis of mothers into witch-like figures reflects an item of Indian psyche. Ashis Nandy observes,

> In terms of organization of personality...the Indian lives in his inner world less with a feared father than with a powerful, aggressive and unreliable mother. Manifestly he idealizes her and sees her as the repository of all nurture and motherliness. Underneath this, there are deep doubts about the nature and the way she might use her powers to aggress. Contrarily, the father is seen as non-interfering, inefficacious, distant and a co-victim of the castrating mother figure (Nandy 107).

In *Midnight's Children*, Naseem gains absolute control over kitchen and subsequently refuses to serve food to her husband and Dr Aziz finds himself to the point of death.

At the dinner table, she continued to rule. No food was set upon the table, no plates were laid. Curry and crockery were marshalled upon a low side table by her right hand, and Dr Aziz and children ate what she dished out. Reverend mother was dismayed when Aziz, her husband had taken control of his children's education. She made only one stipulation: religious instruction. But Aziz threw out the religious tutor because he taught the children a lesson in hate; to hate Hindus, Buddhists, Jains and Sikhs. He asks his wife, 'Will you have hateful children, woman?' To this the reverend mother retorted, 'Will you have Godless ones?' (43). And she retaliates, no food from the kitchen for Aziz until the Maulavi Sahib is back. The war of starvation began and soon became a duel to death.

It appears the reverend mother has alternate roles of a nurturing and destructive woman. She even develops love-hate relationship with her daughters too and occasionally turns uncommunicative if something disagreeable meets the eye. Sometimes she appears to be a comic caricature.

MIAN ABDULLAH

Mian Abdullah is a nationalist Muslim who, along with Aadam Aziz, had been aglow with optimism fever. He had the strange trait of humming without pause. He was called a humming bird and his humming was musical and mechanical. His hum rose and fell in direct relationship to his work rate. His hum could give one toothache and when it rose to its highest, feverish pitch, it did induce erections in anyone within its vicinity. Nadir Khan, his personal secretary was constantly attacked by the master's humming and influenced by his optimism disease.

It was a crucial period in the history of the freedom movement. Congress party and the Muslim League parted ways and partition of the country appeared to be the eventuality. This is a reflection on the negative aspect of the freedom struggle. But Mian Abdullah is one of the patriotic Indians who opposed the partition as demanded by the League on the ground that carving out a pure land for the Muslims will not serve the poor people among the community. He was supported by the patrons like Rani of Cooch Naheen who comments on partition theme,

> 'Landowners with vested interests to protect what do they have to do with Muslims? They go like toads to the British and form Governments for them, now that the Congress refuses to do. They are mad. Otherwise why would they want to partition India?' (47).

Mian Abdullah in the novel is imagined to create the alternative history as opposed to the Congress and Muslim League variety of the official history of compromise on the Two-Nation theory. He created the Free Island Convocation almost single-handedly. He invited the leaders of the dozens of Muslim splinter groups to form a loosely federated alternative to the dogmatism and vested interest of the Leaguers. The first convocation was held in Lahore and the second was held in Agra under the sponsorship of Mian Abdullah. Members of the agrarian movements, urban labourers, and religious divines—all assembled in Agra. There was an opinion that the League with its demand for a partitioned India spoke on nobody's behalf but its own. The assembly under the leadership of Mian Abdullah opposed the partition. But then Agra was a Muslim League stronghold and Mian Abdullah had many enemies.

The anti-partition convocation was held on the campus of Agra University and it was a success. There was a poster on the office wall, expressing Abdullah's favourite anti-partition sentiment, a quote from the poet Iqbal: 'Where can we find a land that is foreign to God?' (49). Abdullah and Nadir were coming to the end of their night's work, the humming bird's hum was low-pitched. There was a knock on the door and Nadir answered it. Six knives held by men dressed in all black, with covered faces, were upon Mian Abdullah. The Humming bird's hum became higher and higher. They say the dogs of the town responded to the humming tune and when they came in large number, Mian Abdullah was dead.

AMINA SINAI

Dr Aziz and 'reverend mother' Naseem Ghani have three daughters, Alice, the eldest, Mumtaz, who is black and Emerald. The three sisters were known in the town as 'the Teen Batti,' the three bright lights. Dr Aziz saw to it that his daughters were exposed to the benefit of modern education notwithstanding his wife's objection. Of these three, Mumtaz who is later known as Amina Sinai after her second marriage with Ahmed Sinai appears to be the best. She, even in her teens is graceful, modest and obedient. She loves her father dearly and always tries to be of comfort to him which he does not get from her mother. She knows that old people need care and attention. She surrenders to her father's wishes when he arranges her marriage with Nadir Khan, a close associate of Mian Abdullah who was killed by the assassins. Nadir Khan left three years after the marriage declaring *Talaaq* (divorce) but Mumtaz maintained her calm and faced her pain with fortitude.

At the instance of her father, Mumtaz re-married. Her new husband Ahmed Sinai was an orphan and later became a merchant. He loved children and so did Mumtaz. After the marriage, Ahmed Sinai chose her a new name, Amina. In the old city of Delhi, Mumtaz reborn as Amina after her second marriage with Ahmed Sinai found her home. As Saleem the narrator observes,

> Dark of skin, glowing of eye, my mother was by nature the most meticulous person on earth. Assiduously, she arranged flowers in the corridors and rooms of the old Delhi house; carpets were selected with infinite care. She could spend twenty-five minutes worrying at the positioning of a chair. By the time she'd finished with her home-making, adding tiny touches here, making fractional alteration there, Ahmed Sinai found her orphan's dwelling transformed into something gentle and loving (74).

She knew that a husband deserves unquestioning loyalty, and unreserved, full-hearted love. She began to train herself to love him notwithstanding her insomnia and her occasional dream of

Nadir Khan, the poet. She divided her husband, mentally, into component parts, physical as well as behavioural. Each day, she selected one fragment of Ahmed Sinai and concentrated her being upon it until it became quite familiar and she felt fondness rising within her and becoming affection and, finally love. She resolved to fall in love with her husband bit by bit. In short she fell under the spell of the perforated sheet of her own parents.

Experience of life made her a philosopher 'Who after all,' she reasoned privately, 'even truly knows another human being completely?' (76). Amina, Ahmed Sinai's loving wife continued to learn to love his appetite for fried foods, his ability to quote Persian poetry, the furrow of anger between his eyebrows. She thought that there would always be something fresh about him to love, 'so our marriage just can't go stale' (76).

Amina has in her all the qualities of a good housewife. Besides, she is a dutiful mother too. This is evident in the episode of one Hindu Lifafa Das beating his dug dugee drum and shouting, 'Dunyadekho' (see the world) who enters the Muslim Muhalla near Chandni Chowk and starts crying his wares in the Sinai's own gully. This was the period of pre-partition violence in Delhi. Hindus and Muslims were at one another's throat. Lifafa Das found himself surrounded by a Muslim mob crying for his blood. Amina saw from her window with dismay a dark shadow between the mob and its Hindu prey with his back against her own doorway. Amina opened her doors and Lifafa fell backwards landing in a dark corridor beside her. She stood there between the mob and its prey, her womb bursting with its invisible secret. Mother in her did rise up to the occasion and Amina shouted at the top of her voice 'Listen, listen well. I am with child. I am a mother who will have a child, and I am giving this man my shelter. Come on now, if you want to kill, kill a mother also and show the world what men you are!' (86).

She is eternal mother and embodies the feminine principle. She is with a child in her womb and the coming of her child in the world was announced to the assembled masses of the people before the father had heard about it. From the moment of its conception, it seems, the child has been public property. Public announcement of the birth of her son saved a life. She was right and wrong at the same time; the baby she was carrying did not turn out to be his son. Amina Sinai is Saleem's mother but not biological mother. The soothsayer's prediction of the birth of a terrible monster does come true, as Saleem with the nose is actually Shiva with the knees. Saleem is the child of the departing colonialist Methwold and the low caste Hindu wife of Willie Winkie, Vanita, who has been changed places at birth, by the nurse Mary Pereira, with Shiva who is really the son of Amina and Ahmed Sinai. Thus Amina, Shiva's biological mother acts as Saleem's mother. A mother is always a mother.

7

Narrative Techniques

Salman Rushdie's second book *Midnight's Children* (1981) introduces innovatory narrative techniques in Indo-Anglian fiction. It is Rushdie who sets the trend for experimentation with narrative technique and usage of the English language. He gave the genre of Indian English fiction a new direction and confidence. The complexity of his narrative technique has attracted the attention of critics. William Walsh observes, 'Combining the elements of magic and fantasy, the grimmest realism, extravagant farce, multi-mirrored analogy and a potent symbolic structure, Salman Rushdie has captured the astonishing energy of the novel unprecedented in scope, manner and achievement in the hundred and fifty-year-old tradition of the Indian novel in English' (Walsh 258).

Prior to Rushdie, technical innovation in respect of Indian English fiction was limited and restricted. Raja Rao was the first to experiment with new narrative techniques in *Kanthapura* (1938). He used a grandmother as a narrator. Kamala Markandaya uses the similar technique in her *Nectar in a Sieve* (1954) where the narrator is a grand-mother. R.K. Narayan uses a flashback technique in *The Guide* (1958). The point of view technique or multiple narrator is used first by Chaman Nahal in *Azadi* (1975), Rushdie's narrative technique in *Midnight's Children* (1981) goes beyond everything hitherto attempted in Indian English fiction. The author Salman Rushdie had been contemplating for long years to write a great story of the Indian subcontinent which as he realized, could not he easily and simplistically rendered. He could recognize the complex nature of the experience of the Indian subcontinent and its social, political and historical realities. The awareness of such realities is paralleled by an awareness of the world of magic and spirituality which defied logical and realistic narrative. The narrative of *Midnight's Children* is open-ended. The author dispensed with linear narrative and the omniscient author tradition as he provides a compelling account of seventy-five years of the history of the Indian subcontinent. The narrative technique of *Midnight's Children* cannot be easily categorized. It can be read as a significant political history and it is not just a political history rather a fantasy novel too. The critics read the text as a 'Non-fiction Novel' and also as a 'political allegory' (Banerjee 195). The narrator Saleem Sinai is eccentric and the narrative drifts into dream, nightmare and fantasy. The narrator of *Midnight's Children* tends to see himself in both the first and third person and hence the reality of the character remains marred. The narrative technique blurs the chronological boundaries. The unities of time and place are also not stable. Novel's narrative technique helps the narrator who is also a chronicler to present the variety and multitudinousness of the life of the subcontinent. As Rushdie's counterpart, Saleem narrates his story from a distance of time and place. Like the narrator of the *Mahabharata,* Sanjay who is endowed with special power to see things from a distance and narrate the events of the Kurukshetra war, Saleem is endowed with magical power so that he can see from a distance and read the minds of others. Saleem like Tristram is the self-conscious narrator, aware of himself as writer. In the case of Saleem and Tristram, the distance the narrator travels may be intellectual. It may be physical or temporal; many novelistic authors are distant from even the most knowing narrators.

In *Midnight's Children* Rushdie has created something genuinely new. Saleem like Tristram is really trying to tell a story, the story of his life and the life of the new nation. His life has been badly shaped by the time, exact hours of his begetting, the confusion of his parentage and a variety of other disasters peculiar to him. With such a narrator in charge of the story-telling our expectation of comic catastrophe is, of course different from that in comic novels like *Tom Jones*. The telling of his story is comic chiefly because there is nothing in the nature of the subject, which may pass for materials for a conventional comic novel. The chaos, if any, is of his own making. The reader is always aware of the existence of a simple chronology of events from 1947 to 1976 that could be told in hundred pages.

Saleem, the narrator enjoys an intellectual distance and hence he requires assistance from a plebeian commentator, to temper his erudition. In *Midnight's Children* the role of the commentator is performed by Saleem's servant and mistress Padma who is not part of the story proper but she participates with Saleem in composing the story. Her relationship is not with Saleem, the character but with Saleem, the narrator. She literally intervenes in the composition of the novel by presenting her comments. Padma supplements the narrative design of the book. She may certainly be considered a literary critic and her authority rests on her being a member of the lower classes. She is not a passive receptor or a disembodied voice of the tradition or popular aesthetics; her role is that of the participant and commentator. Padma's role in the narrative is the author's 'playful acknowledgement of a tradition of national literature which his peripheral status allows him to criticize even as he participates in it' (Brennan 101).

Saleem Sinai bears parallel with 18th century narrator Tristram in the sense that both write under impotence which is metaphorical. Saleem's birth at the midnight hour brought him into collision with the political forces. As a result, he has been unmanned forever by the minions of the leader he calls widow. The narrator's identification of the widow constitutes the point at which his narrative begins to transgress the boundaries of the fiction, Saleem states his widow-induced castration to Padma, which has a political overtone. Thus he provides her with the reason for his impotence and his status as the fictional Saleem.

> But Padma knows what I can no longer do; Padma, who once, in her anger, cried out: 'But what use are you, my God, as a lover?' That part, at least, can be

> verified: in the hovel of Picture Singh, I cursed myself with the lie of impotence.... (440)

Like King Shahryar in *A Thousand and One Nights*, Padma takes pity on her narrative suitor. But then Padma's superstitious nature links her with the widow who is 'obsessed with stars' (427). Saleem's sexual impotence is the price he pays for political awareness. Padma, the naratee is politically ignorant and thus ineffective. Saleem's sexual impotence also becomes a metaphor for his political impotence. 'Padma is not the widow. Saleem has missed the spittoon' (Batty 109).

The tension between Padma's 'what happened nextism' (39) and Saleem's need to conceal, shapes the entire narrative to a large extent. "But here is Padma at my elbow, bullying me back into the world of linear narrative, the universe of what happened next. 'At this rate,' Padma complains, 'you'll be two hundred years old before you manage to tell about your birth.'" Saleem explains to her that he must go back two generations to tell his own story because 'the past has dripped into me...so we can't ignore it...' her shrug, cuts me off. 'To me it's a crazy way of telling your life-story,' she cries, 'if you can't even get to where your father met your mother.' Padma's 'ministrations are also her aesthetic interference; her solicitations are both petitions and harangues' (Brennan 104). Saleem, the narrator rejects Padma's aesthetic counsels which condition the narrative but do not dictate the form.

Padma's plebeian strength of storytelling is echoed by some other characters. Mary Pereira's gift for preserving memories may be compared to Padma's making of chutney (*MC* 252). The boatman Tai's chatter says the narrator 'was fantastic, grandiloquent and ceaseless' (*MC* 9). His age no one could remember, his verbiage was endless and his talk magical and he was illiterate. Tai's store of memory keeps the community aware of its past. 'Tai-for-changelessness opposed to Adam-for-progress' (*MC* 124). Thus Padma, the narrator's female audience represents aesthetically 'earthiness of spirit' (*MC* 124) as well as ignorance, superstition and love of the fabulous which characterize the life of the gullible folk. The erudite narrator is not supposed to reject her crudeness on the ground of his own sophistication. Politically, Padma's lower class impulses in art metaphorically state the fatal immaturity of her class in the struggle for meaningful freedom. She is gullible and resents any breaking of the narrative spell.

> I must interrupt myself. I wasn't going to today because Padma has started getting irritated whenever my narration becomes self-conscious, whenever like an incompetent puppeteer, I reveal the hands holding the strings (*MC* 72).

She advocates instead 'The world of linear narrative, the universe of what happened next' (38).. It appears, being an illiterate, she is 'jealous of written words', Saleem, the narrator gives more time to writing than to her, and she is unable to resuscitate his 'other pencil' (141). But the fact remains that Padma is Saleem's typical audience his 'necessary ear' (177) and his principal critic. She brings to surface the thoughts of the readers. Aesthetically speaking, she provides an image of the Indian masses 'gullibility.' Saleem refers to her unquestioning faith in his narrative. 'I vouchsafe daily glimpses of myself—while she, my squatting glimpser, is captivated, helpless as a monogoose frozen into immobility by the swaying, blinkless eyes of a hooded snake' (142). Her gullibility (folkloric simplicity) may be construed as her inability and failure to challenge the demagogy of India's post-Independence leaders. Thus notwithstanding the unreliability of the narrator, his errors of memory, inconsistencies of plot, Saleem, the narrator is assured that Padma will believe his story. His writing turns out to be a process of imposing his vision of truth on others. He observes cynically, 'In all literature, what actually happened is less important than what the author can manage to persuade his audience to believe' (325). The narrator becomes the creator of the fictional universe. He may be seen as a poet who imagines things. *Apāra visvasamsāre kabireba prajāpati.* Narrator can be imagined as Brahma, the *Prajāpati.*

It is said that the narrator Saleem contains within himself '630 million particles of oblivious dust' (37) one for each soul, of the Indian masses whose terrible force threatens to destroy him. He must record his tale before he explodes (which he does in the final pages). His tale should not be lost to the world after he dies. He learns the technique of pickling from Padma, his lover and audience. Her boiling pots of chutney remain always within the smelling reach of Saleem's writing desk. As the narrator records his fictional accounts of Indian history for posterity, each chapter corresponds to one of the twenty-six pickle jars he adds to the shelf beside his writing desk. The novel *MC* thus remains what Rushdie calls a 'chutnification of history.' Keeper of the pickle jars above Saleem's writing table, Padma, the narratee, is naturally a preserver of tradition. But she does not possess memory, which is historical quality and which is at odds with the repetitive logic of folklore. Rushdie makes the distinction between history and folklore, the narrator and the narratee clear at the point when Saleem counterposes his own 'wild God of memory' to Padma's 'lotus Goddess of the present?' (177). At other point, she dismisses the past as so much 'funny tack' (531). If Padma represents linear narrative and the universe of 'what happened next' she does so because she remains arrested in a world of immediate sensation, without interest in history and criticism. And this is just what the 'Midnight-Confidential clubs'—the degenerate form of the Parliament of India—comes to represent 'Here you are in a world without faces or names; here people have no memories, families or past, here is for now' (541). The alternate agreement and antagonism between Padma and Saleem (symbolically represented by their inability to consummate sexual union) reflects the ambivalent relationship of literature and folklore, of upper and lower classes, of Eastern and Western influences. The national longing for form of the narrative does not necessarily mean a longing for nationhood but a 'parody on the level of imaginative form, of ridiculously disparate social elements yoked together unsuccessfully (Propp 8). In an important sense the narrative provides space for post-modernity because parody, burlesque, comicality and discontinuity define a post-modern text. In *Midnight's Children* the narrator deliberately breaks continuity by interrupting the narrative with items of history. These interruptions are presented in the shape of 'Public

Announcements,' illusions of Bombay Cinema or thought control methods (All India Radio). The aim of the narrator is to protect the audience from the tyranny of the narrative by breaking the narrative spell and thus to constitute a formal assault on orderly fictions and linear narrative. The challenge of Saleem's narrative project is to create a fiction that will do justice to multiple realities or alternative realities: myth, history memory, languages, post-colonial politics and so on. At one point, Saleem refers to the 'two threads' of the narrative, 'The thread that leads to the ghetto of the magicians; and the thread that tells the story of Nadir the rhymeless, verbless poet' (*MC* 46).

Saleem's narrative or rather counter-narrative makes a juxtaposition of the public and the private, the historical and the biographical. This kind of narrative strategy informs the writings of Plutarch, Shakespeare and Walter Scott. In *Midnight's Children*, the event of the birth of a nation is paralleled by the birth of the central character Saleem Sinai who is the first person narrator. 1001 magical children are born in that historical hour of the midnight of August 15, 1947. The narrator Saleem appears to be the representative of the magical children and is a great storyteller. He tells his unending story to his listener, the simple woman, as they work together in the pickle-factory, his is an act of narrative which provides a metaphor for the fictional process itself. The narrator/narratee paradigm is a fortunate innovation. It is the relationship between Padma and Saleem, narratee and narrator, made up of her interruption and his evasions, that provides the point of entry for the reader into the narrative and sustains interest till the end. Commentary and digressions provide the sauce to the narrative and in Saleem's case, his writing is also an act of conversation.

Thus in the middle of the novel, at the 'Alpha and Omega' chapter (16) Saleem announces 'my story's half-way point' looking both back and forwards: 'there are beginnings here, and all manners of ends' (*MC* 218). As we have already visited the end of the story, 'It is morning at the pickle factory; they have brought my son to see me...someone speaks anxiously, trying to force her way into my story ahead of time' (*MC* 205), so when we come near the actual conclusion the earlier scenes are recycled. In the chapter 28 'A Wedding,' Saleem explains to Padma his marriage to Parvati-the-witch only by linking this back to the story of all the women in his life, beginning in a 'blind landowner's house on the shores of a Kashmiri lake' with Naseem Aziz his unmarried grandmother (*MC* 391-92). 'Once upon a time,' 'I have told this story before' (*MC* 209, 212, 354), the phrases borrowed from oral narrative recur through the novel and animate the texture of the narrative.

Let us have a close look at the structure of the narrative. Saleem is born at midnight on 15 August 1947—'at the precise instant of India's arrival at independence, I tumbled forth into the world' (*MC* 11). In chapter 14 'My tenth birthday,' 'freak weather storms, floods, hailstones from a cloudless sky—manage to wreck the second Five Year plan' and on the same day Saleem establishes 'my very own M.C.C.—the new Midnight Children's Conference' (*MC* 202-03). He uses newspaper cuttings from the year 1960 to compose the fatal communication to commander Sabarmati revealing his wife's affairs and explains this as 'my first attempt at re-arranging history' (*MC* 262-63). The conversational ebb and flow of his address is amply demonstrated in the chapter 17 'The Kolynos kid.' Saleem as a man of science, states his claim to a place at the centre of things. He desires to be heard. 'I was linked to history both literally and metaphorically, both actively and passively, in what our scientists might term' modes of connection composed of 'dualistically-combined configurations' (232). Saleem's claims sound ironical and have a distancing effect. The narrative conducts a negotiation between fact and fiction in the novel which has been rightly described by Andrzej Gasiorek:

> *Midnight's Children* is a double voice narrative in which a personal discourse of self-discovery interacts with, and is constrained by a public discourse of history and politics. It persistently admonishes those who either succumb to private fantasies about the world or distort it for political purposes. Rushdie's narrative mode does not seek to do away with the distinction between fantasy and reality but shows how

> strange and unstable was the political reality of the time.

The observation of Gasiorek bears relevance with our reading of the chapter 21 'Drainage and Desert', where there is an ironic correspondence between Saleem's own life story so far and the progress of the Indo-Chinese border war of 1962 (*MC* 286-87). In the same vein, we are invited to believe that 'the hidden purpose of the Indo-Pakistan war of 1965 was nothing more or less than the elimination of my benighted family from the fact of the earth (*MC* 327). Subsequent events in history drag Saleem to conflict. "The belligerent events of 1971, the Civil War in Pakistan, deliver him up as a guide in the Pakistani army, prompting his disappearance into the Sundarbans and his reappearance seven months later into the world of armies and dates" (*MC* 356). India's first nuclear explosion in May 1974 coincides with the return of the war like Shiva (Saleem's anti-self) into the narrative. The protracted labour of Parvati to deliver her child Aadam parallels the period of thirteen days in June 1975 between the returning of the guilty verdict on Mrs Gandhi and her seizure of emergency powers (*MC* 420-24). Saleem the narrator himself becomes a victim 'of the sterilization programme along with other midnight's children. Metaphorically the forceful sterilization means the nullity of the hopes and possibilities with which they were born.

The relationship between history and lived experience becomes problematised when the narrator introduces the factual errors into the narrative. The reader is warned against uncritical reading. Rushdie's own essay, 'Unreliable narration in *Midnight's Children*' throws light on this issue. 'Using memory as our tool ...we remake the past to suit our present purposes.' Saleem's story remains exemplary: 'The reading of Saleem's unreliable narration might be...a useful analogy for the way in which we all, everyday, attempt to read the world (*IH* 24-25). Saleem confesses that 're-reading my work, I have discovered an error in chronology.' 'The assassination of Mahatma Gandhi occurs, in these pages on the wrong date. And this now cannot be corrected: In my India, Gandhi will continue to die at wrong time' (*MC* 164). The error prompts the narrator's question:

'Does one error invalidate the entire fabric? Am I so far gone, in my desperate need for meaning, that I'm prepared to distort everything—to rewrite the whole history of my times purely in order to place myself in a central role?' (*MC* 164). It is left for the reader to judge. 'There is always more to history than the facts. Some legends make reality, and become more useful than the facts' (*MC* 47).

The narrative aims to 'build reality' from scraps of information (*MC* 412) and *Midnight's Children* is solidly built of facts and figures, dates and events from Amritsar, Bangladesh and Bhopal to Queen Victoria, two world wars and General Zia. But the story we end up with will be conditional, open at both ends. Imagination has its own rules. The reader has been warned against its capacity for error and distortion. The subjective view is unreliable because of the fallibility of our perceptions and memories. Rushdie's narrative point of view is typically epic and externalized and the novel *Midnight's Children* is not a psychological novel either. The narrator is nevertheless acutely aware of the unpredictability of our cognitive process and the fragility of 'the mind's divisions between fantasy and reality' (*MC* 165). This also was a central theme of *Grimus* and also *The Satanic Verses*.

8

Style, Trope and Symbol

Rushdie's major post-colonial text *Midnight's Children* grapples with the ideas of 'nation' and 'history.' The concept that nations are invented or the definition of nation as an 'imagined community' have gained wide acceptance following the works of Anderson, Eric Hobsbawn *et al.* With Rushdie, the concept of nation is fictionalized and narrated imaginatively in *Midnight's Children*, and entirely new symbols and devices came into existence. There takes place the personification of 'the nation' in symbols, images, metaphors and tropes.

According to the book's major trope, Saleem contains within himself '630 million particles of oblivious dust' (37) one for each soul of the Indian masses whose terrible force threatens to destroy him. He is, therefore, in a hurry to record his tale before he explodes. The narrator is anxious to preserve his memory from decay and he learns from Padma, the female narratee, the techniques of pickling. Her boiling pots of chutney are displayed throughout the tale so that the pots or pickling jars remain within the smelling reach of Saleem's writing desk. The text *Midnight's Children* may be read as a history and each new chapter of the post-colonial history corresponds to one of the twenty-six pickle jars. It is said and said rightly that *Midnight's Children* is a 'chutnification of history.'

Description of the love affair between Lila Hindustan and Homi Catrack which is compared to those of several legendary lovers, exemplifies what Timothy Brannon terms Rushdie's 'encyclopaedic style' (Brannon 107) 'Once upon a time there were Radha and Krishna, and Rama and Sita, and Laila and

Majnu...' (311). What is emphasized here is an inescapable pattern of behaviour codified in the ancient myth, classical Indian myth is useful in respect of an appropriate national style. Through the characterization of the primary mythical figures, Rushdie's novel *Midnight's Children* tries to satisfy the 'national' longing for form.' Parvati, Shiva and Ganesh each represent distinct aspects of the national style found in *Midnight's Children*. Fictional Parvati is a resident of the 'ghetto of magicians' and 'the conjurers slum' filled with 'fakirs' and 'illusionists.' Her powers of sorcery can make appear real what is not. Illusion appears through *Midnight's Children* in specifically Indian form. There is popular linking of magic and Eastern mysticism. Ramram Seth is Indian soothsayer and so is Lord Khusru and there is India's national medium of illusion—the Bombay Cinema. Padma's symbolical role of plebian commentator and her insistence on what-happens-nextism has been rejected by the narrator and this rejection is found in the aesthetic influence of Ganesh who is an offspring of Shiva and Parvati. Besides, Ganesh is also Saleem's figurative 'son' (Aadam) who represents the culmination of national style. Elephant-headed Ganesh serves as the medium and through him the entire story is filtered. Is not Saleem, the narrator, born with an elephantine nose and his son (Shiva's biological son) born with elephantine ears? In an important way Ganesh provides the culmination of national style. This is an Indian disease, 'this urge to encapsulate the whole of reality' (84). Lifafa Das, the peepshow man cries out as he walks the streets of Delhi displaying his collection of picture postcards, 'see the whole world, come see everything' (83). It is from this unique Indian perspective to contain the whole world (Nālpe sukham asti, bhūmaiba sukham) that Rushdie develops his attack on linearity. Saleem admits his being 'a swallower of lives' in which 'consumed multitudes are jostling and shoving' (4). Mujeebuddin Syed sees the escape from linear time in *Midnight's Children* in terms of the cyclic notions of *Kala* and *Laya* and he connects the trope of cracking and disintegration to the dismemberment of the primeval male (*purusha*). The assertion of oneness of man with God and a state of madness or fever (Saleem's fever in the text) associated with religious exaltation in Sufism are explained as elements that go into the imaginative structure of the novel. In fact, as Mujeebuddin has shown, the mode of magical realism gives Rushdie ample scope to move between the modernist and post-modernist vis-à-vis the folklorist tradition of India and the narrator incorporates a complex web of Hindu, Islamic and German motifs, the philosophy of *Maya* and *karma* and Sufism.[1]

The formal assault on orderly fiction as Timothy Brennan maintains, 'provides the only way out of Saleem-Shiva duality' (Brennan 117). It is precisely their rivalry that produces the third element—Ganesh whose style expresses a chaotic 'sum total of everything'—which constitutes an appropriate paradigm for India's national form in respect of her unique diversity and all-inclusiveness. In other words, duality between Shiva and Saleem may suggest thesis and anti-thesis while Ganesh borders on synthesis. Neither Saleem nor Padma singly can create true national image because post-colonial nationalism is international.

NOTE

1. Syed Mujeebuddin. *Midnight's Children and its Indian con-texts* in Meenakshi Mukherjee (ed.) *Rushdie's Midnight's Children—A Book of Readings*, Pencraft International Delhi, 2003. The mode of magical or fabulous realism offers Rushdie freedom to move between modernist/ post modernist and the folkloric tradition of India. The narrator dishes out a hybrid tale of India incorporating a complex web of Hindu, Islamic and Christian motifs, the philosophy of *Maya* and *Karma* and Sufism.

WORK CITED

Brennan, Timothy. *Salman Rushdie and the Third World*, Macmillan, London, 1989.

9

Critical Reception of *Midnight's Children*

There are two distinct camps in the diverse body of writing that constitutes Rushdie studies. In the one camp are those writers and critics who believe that Rushdie's tendency to incorporate and rework previous systems of writing is commendable because it permits him to dismantle the master's house using master's own tools. In the other camp are those who argue that Rushdie in establishing his oppositional politics in relation to colonial modes of writing identifies post-colonialism as a political form that only revalidates, a colonialist centre. The position held by the former post-structuralist camp is strengthened by a new study made by Jaina C. Sanga in her book *Salman Rushdie's Post-Colonial Metaphors: Migration, Translation, Hybridity, Blasphemy and Globalisation*. The book examines the fact that Rushdie's fictional narratives are subversive in that these narrative acts disrupt obsolete colonial system of thinking in order to create new post-colonial systems that revolutionise our understanding of nation, nationalism, culture and identity. Sanga believes that it is through metaphorical experience that political opposition is presented in the Rushdie text, the colonial discourse establishes its political urgency through certain metaphors like 'bringing light and civilization to the dark places in the world.' Post-colonial counter-discourse uses alternative metaphorical formulations of its own. Patrick Brantlinger, Sara Suleri and Robert Young have examined the demythologization of colonialist metaphors. Sanga focuses upon five metaphors in Rushdie's fiction. These are migration, translation, hybridity, blasphemy and globalization. The post-colonial metaphors in a peculiarly Rushdiesque way tend to problematize 'entrenched versions of reality.' Now the trope of blasphemy remains Rushdie's principal *modus operandi* because Rushdie is a writer who persistently challenges settled notions and remains offensive to entrenched interests. It may be the blasphemy of a satirist who in the line of Swift, critiques in order to liberate.

There are criticisms of Rushdie from Islamic perspective. Shabbir Akhtar advances the arguments that texts like *Satanic Verses* (1988) may reinforce prejudice against a Muslim minority. Ziauddin Sardar argues that "the West's secular liberal conception of freedom of speech actually serves to dominate other cultures who may not wholly subscribe to these notions" (Sanga 126). Post-structuralist critics like Sanga offer a defense of freedom of speech in literature citing Rabelais, Swift and Joyce and maintain that one of the main tasks of post-colonial writing has been the 'interrogation of Western colonial discourse' (76). Rushdie's unique use of language has attracted the attention of these post-structuralist critics who share Rushdie's own theoretical framework and hold that it is through language that our reality is constructed and it is 'written in system of language that all discourses, social, cultural and political are grounded' (Sanga 50).

On the other hand, Harish Trivedi is one of the negative critics of Rushdie who is less impressed by the alleged subversiveness of Rushdie's language and criticizes the authorial claim that 'conquering' the English language through infiltration is a strategic step towards decolonization. Trivedi observes that occasional sprinkling of Hindi-Urdu-Hindustani words and phrases in *Midnight's Children* does not alter 'the basic ingredients of the English curry'. He further observes, 'To use the master's language is immitigably to speak in the master's voice.' Critics Aijaz Ahmad and Kumkum Sangari do not believe that Rushdie's mode of political critique is the primary mode available to politicized thinkers who represent once colonized nations. Aijaz Ahmad in his famous book *In Theory* maintains that post-structuralist post-colonial literature and theory in the western canon is a neocolonial mechanism designed to maintain a westernized and othering vision of the 'East.' Critics like Ahmad, Sangari and now Graham Huggan do not share Rushdie's theoretical framework and reject the Foucauldian assumptions about power and resistance.

But then Rushdie's use of the carnivalesque and fantastic European traditions might be interpreted as a 'desire for metropolitan western acceptance.' Roger Clark's new study of Rushdie *Stranger Gods: Salman Rushdie's Other Worlds* is a different kind of Rushdie study altogether. Clark makes a detailed elucidation of the meaning of names and places in Rushdie text in the light of the *Koran*, Norse myth or Persian poetry. His explication of the symbolism in the Sundarbans episode of *Midnight's Children* in relation to Islamic ideas of heaven and Hindu ideas of hell is illuminating. But the fact remains that the spiritual and mystical models employed by Rushdie are used not for any transcendentalist meaning but for political or theoretical allegories. References to Farid-ud-Din Attar's *Conference of the Birds* in Rushdie's fiction may be understood as a potent satire on political power and allows the author to explore the conceptions of migrancy and community. Rushdie's revisitations of the 'unity' that the birds attain in Attar's poems may be understood as wilful subversion of Attar's unifying vision that concern instead with notions of disseminated nationhood theorized by critics like Homi Bhabha. Rushdie's *Midnight's Children* remains one of the greatest classics of twentieth century. A question that arises is: Will Rushdie remain an important writer in the twenty first? Mixed reception of his later works suggests that his distinction is less than assured. But there are critics who believe that Rushdie's continual analysis of post-imperial and neo-imperial situations and his analysis of the trends and tendencies of globalization, multinationalism and post-nationalism will surely make him a significant voice for the future.

10

Some Model Questions

Broad answer type questions

1. Comment on the title of the novel, *Midnight's Children*. In what way does the title refer to post-colonial India?
2. Discuss the major themes and issues of the text *Midnight's Children*.
3. Analyze the narrative technique as employed by the writer in the text *Midnight's Children*.
4. Discuss the use of major symbols and tropes in the text *Midnight's Children*.
5. Discuss in brief Rushdie's art of characterization.
6. How far are Rushdie's personal experience and his response to India embodied in the novel?
7. Discuss role of narrator hero in the novel *Midnight's Children*.
8. Critically analyze Rushdie's attempt at fictionalizing the epical figure 'Ganesh' in the novel.
9. Write a critical note on the minor characters of *Midnight's Children*.
10. Comment on Rushdie's comic treatment of post-colonial Indian history or fictionalizing the post-partition history of the subcontinent.
11. Write a critical note on the role of Padma, Saleem's female narratee.
12. Critically analyze Rushdie's treatment of women characters in the novel.

13. Compare and contrast the characters of Saleem and Shiva in terms of the circumstances of birth and the major functions they are made to perform in the text.
14. Consider *Midnight's Children* as a post-modern novel.
15. What is magic realism? Write in brief on Rushdie's use of magic realism in the novel.

Short answer type questions

1. Comment briefly on the role of the nurse Mary Pareira.
2. Write a few lines on Rushdie's metaphorical use of the expression 'knees is nose and nose is knees.'
3. Comment on the significance of the perforated sheet.
4. What does Boatman Tai stand for in the novel? Write in brief.
5. Why Padma is called 'the dung lotus'?
6. Who is reverend mother in the novel and why is she so-called?
7. Comment on the statement Saleem was 'handcuffed to history' at birth.
8. Write in brief the symbolic significance of Lifafa Das's 'Dugdugee Drum' and his announcement 'Duniya Dekho.'
9. Why were the midnight's children subjected to forced sterilization during Emergency?
10. How was Saleem transported to India from Bangladesh?
11. Comment on Saleem's experience in the Sundarban forest.
12. What is the symbolic significance of Sundarban episode?
13. Comment on Saleem's parentage.
14. Examine the significance of M.C.C.

Select Bibliography

Ahmad, Aizaz. *In Theory*. London: Verso, 1992.

Akhtar, Shabbir. *Be Careful with Muhammad! The Salman Rushdie Affair*. London: Bellow, 1989.

Ali, Tariq. "Review of *Midnight's Children*," *New Left Review*: 136 (1982): 87-95.

Amanuddin, Syed. "The Novels of Salman Rushdie," *World Literature Today*: 63 (1) (1989): 42-45.

Banerjee, Ashutosh. "Narrative Technique in *Midnight's Children*," *Three Contemporary Novelists*. (ed.) Dr R.K. Dhawan. Delhi: 1985.

Batty, Nancy E. "The Art of Suspense" in *Rushdie's Midnight's Children*. Ed. Meenakshi Mukherjee. Delhi: 2003, 95-111

Benedict, Anderson. *Imagined Communities*. London: Verso, 1983.

Bharucha, Rustom. "Rushdie's *Whale*," *The Massachusetts Review*: 27(2) (1986): 221-37.

Birch, David. "Post-modern Chutneys," *Textual Practice*: 5 (1) (1991): 1-7.

Branttiner, Patrick. *Rule of Darkness, British Literature and Imperialism 1830-1914*. Ithaca: Cornell UP, 1988.

Brennan, Timothy. *Salman Rushdie and the Third World: Myths of the Nation*. London: Macmillan, 1989.

Brooks, David. "Interview with Rushdie," *Helix* 19 (1984).

Candy, Catherine. *Salman Rushdie*. Manchester: Manchester University Press, 1996.

Clark, Roger Y. *Stranger Gods: Salman Rushdie's Other Worlds*. Montreal: McGill-Queen's UP, 2001.

D'Souza, Florence. "Salman Rushdie's *Midnight's Children*: A Remythologisation of India's Contemporary History," *Salman Rushdie Critical Essays,* (eds.) Mohit K. Ray and Rama Kundu. New Delhi: Atlantic Publishers & Distributors (P) Ltd., Vol. 1, 2006, 34-49.

Desai, Anita. Personal Interview, S. Hadley, Massachusetts, November 1972.

Dingwaney, Anuradha. "Author(iz)ing *Midnight's Children and Shame*" in S. Emanuel Nelson (ed.), *Reworlding: The Literature of the Indian Diaspora*. Westport: Greenwood, 1992, 157-68.

Durix, Jean-Pierre. "Magic Realism in *Midnight's Children*," *Commonwealth Essays and Studies*: 8 (1) (1985): 57-63.

Flanagan, Kathleen. "The Fragmented Self in Salman Rushdie's *Midnight's Children*," *Commonwealth Novel in English*: 5 (1) (1992): 38-45.

Fletcher, M.D. (ed.). *Reading Rushdie: Perspectives on the Fiction of Salman Rushdie*. Amsterdam: Rodopi, 1994.

Ghosh, Tapan Kumar (ed.). *Salman Rushdie's Midnight's Children*. New Delhi: Asia Book Club, 2004.

Goonetileke, D.C.R.A. *Salman Rushdie*. London: Macmillan, 1998.

Grant, Danian. *Writers and Their Work*. North Cote House in association with British Council. UK: Plymouth, 1999.

Harrison, James. "Reconstructing *Midnight's Children* and *Shame*," *University of Toronto Quarterly*: 59 (3) (1990): 399-412.

Harrison, James. *Salman Rushdie*. New York: Twayne Publishers, 1992.

Hewson, Kelly. "Opening up the Universe a Little More: Salman Rushdie and the Migrant as Story-teller," *SPAN* (Journal of the South Pacific Association for Commonwealth Literature and Language Studies): 29 (1989): 82-93.

Huggan, Graham. "The Post-colonial Exotic: Salman Rushdie and the Booker of Books," *Transition*, 64 (1994): 22-29.

Kanaganayakam, C. "Myth and Fabulosity in *Midnight's Children.*" *Dalhousie Review*: 67 (1) (1987): 86-98.

Kene, Jean M. "The Migrant Intellectual and the Body of History: Salman Rushdie's *Midnight's Children*," *Contemporary Literature*: 37 (1) (1996): 94-117.

Magnusson, Magnus and Rosemary Goring (eds.). *The Cambridge Biographical Dictionary*. New York: Cambridge UP, 1990, 12.

Morrison, Blake. "An Interview with Salman Rushdie," *Granta* 31 (1990) (Spring).

Mujeebuddin, Syed. *Midnight's Children and its Indian Contexts* in *Rushdie's Midnight's Children—A Book of Readings*, (ed.). Meenakshi Mukherjee. Delhi: Pencraft International, 2003, 149-64.

Mukherjee, Arun. "Characterization in Salman Rushdie's *Midnight's Children*: Breaking Out of the Hold of Realism and Seeking the 'Alienation Effect'" in Viney Kirpal (ed.), *The New Indian Novel in English: A Study of the 1980s*. New Delhi: Allied Publishers, 1990, 109-19.

Mukherjee, Meenakshi (ed.). *Rushdie's Midnight's Children*, Delhi, 2003.

Nandy, Ashis. *At the Edge of Psychology: Essays in Politics & Culture*. New Delhi: OUP, 1980.

Natarajan, Nalini. "Woman, Nation and Narration in *Midnight's Children*" in *Rushdie's Midnight's Children—A Book of Readings*. Ed. Meenakshi Mukherjee. Delhi: Pencraft, International, 2003, 165-81.

Noor, Ronny. "Misrepresentation of History in Salman Rushdie's *Midnight's Children*," *Notes on Contemporary Literature*: 26 (2) 1996, 7-8.

Parameshwaran, Uma. "Handcuffed to History: Salman Rushdie's Art," *Ariel:* 14 (1983): 34-45.

Parameshwaran, Uma. *The Perforated Sheet: Essays on Salman Rushdie's Art*. Madras: Affiliated East-West Press, 1988.

Paterson, Margareta. *Unending Metamorphoses: Myth, Satire and Religion in Salman Rushdie's Novels*. Lund (Sweden): Lund University Press, 1996.

Price, David. "Salman Rushdie's Use and Abuse of History in *Midnight's Children*," *Ariel:* 25 (2) (1994): 91-107.

Propp, Vladimir. *Theory and History of Folklore*. Ed. Anatoly Liberman. Minnesota Press, 1984.

Rao, Madhusudhana. *Salman Rushdie's Fiction: A Study (Satanic Verses Excluded)*, New Delhi: Sterling Publishers, 1992.

Ray, Mohit K. and Rama Kundu (Eds.). *Salman Rushdie: Critical Essays,* 2 Vols. New Delhi: Atlantic Publishers and Distributors (P) Ltd., 2002.

Rege, Josna E. "Victim into Protagonist? *Midnight's Children* and the Post-Rushdie National Narratives of the Eighties" quoted in Meenakshi Mukherjee (ed.). *Midnight's Children: A Book of Readings*. Delhi: Pencraft International, 2003. 183-208.

Reimenschneider, Dieter. "History and the Individual in Anita Desai's *Clear Light of Day* and *Salman Rushdie's Midnight's Children*," *World Literature Written in English:* 23 (1) (1994): 196-207, Reprinted in Viney Kirpal (ed.). *The New Indian Novel in English*, New Delhi: Allied Publishers, 1990, 187-99.

Rushdie, Salman (ed). *Imaginary Homelands: Essays and Criticism*, Harmondsworth, Penguin, 1981-91.

Rushdie, Salman. "Imaginary Homelands," *Essays and Criticism 1981-1991*, New York, Viking, 1991.

Rushdie, Salman, *Midnight's Children*. 1981, London: Picador, 1982.

Rushdie, Salman, *Midnight's Children*. 1981, London: Picador, 1982. All page references are to this edition *Imaginary Homelands: Essays and Criticism 1981-1991*, London, Granta 1991.

Rushdie, Salman. "Interview with Salman Rushdie" by C. Pattanayak, *The Literary Criticism* XVIII, 1983.

Rushdie, Salman. Interview. Kunnapipi 7 (1985): 17.

Rushdie, Salman. Interview. Kunnapipi: 1985.

Rushdie, Salman. *Midnight's Children and Shame* (Lecture/ Interview). Kunnapipi 7 (1) (1985): 1-19.

Rushdie, Salman. *Midnight's Children.* 1981, London: Vintage (1991, 1995). All page references are to this edition.

Sanga, Jaina C. *Salman Rushdie's Post-Colonial Metaphors.* Westport, CT: Greenwood, 2001.

Sangari, Kumkum. "The Politics of the Possible," *Cultural Critique:* 7 (1987).

Sardar, Jiauddin & Merryl Davis. *Distorted Imaginations.* London: Grey Seal, 1970.

Slemon, Stephen. "Magic Realism as Post-Colonial Discourse," *Canadian Literature:* 116 (1988): 9-24.

Srivastava, Aruna. "The Empire Writes Back: Language and History in *Midnight's Children,*" *Ariel*: 20 (4) (1989): 62-78.

Stephens, John. "*Midnight's Children*: The Parody of an Indian Novel," *SPAN* (Journal of the South Pacific Association for Commonwealth Literature and Language Studies): 21 (1985): 184-208.

Suleri, Sora. *The Rhetoric of English India.* Chicago, 1992.

Swann, Joseph. "'East is East and West is West?' Salman Rushdie's *Midnight's Children* as an Indian Novel," *World Literature Written in English:* 26 (2) (1986): 353-62. Reprinted in Viney Kirpal (ed.), *The New Indian Novel in English.* New Delhi: Allied Publishers, 1990, 251-61.

Tyssens, Stephanie. "*Midnight's Children* or the Ambiguity of Impotence," *Commonwealth Essays and Studies:* 12 (1) (1989): 19-29.

Verman, Charu. "Padma's Tragedy," *PURBA* (Punjab University Research Bulletin-Arts): 20 (2) (1989): 56-65.

Walsh, William. "Indian and the Novel," *The New Pelican Guide to English Literature: The Present.* Ed. Boris Ford. Penguin, 1983.

Wilson, Keith. "*Midnight's Children* and Reader Responsibility," *Critical Quarterly*: 26 (3) (1984): 23-37.

Young, Robert. *Colonial Desire: Hybridity in Theory*. New York: Routledge, 1995.

Index

D

E

F

G